THE ILLUSTRATED

KamaSutra

ANANGA-RANGA · PERFUMED GARDEN

'The yoni is cool, hard, fleshy, yet delicate; and there is love and regard for the husband. Such is . . . the highest temperament' (Central India).

THE ILLUSTRATED
KAMA SUTRA

ANANGA-RANGA · PERFUMED GARDEN

THE CLASSIC EASTERN LOVE TEXTS

The SIR RICHARD BURTON and
F. F. Arbuthnot translations
edited and introduced by
Charles Fowkes

HAMLYN

Text

EDITOR'S NOTE All three works have been substantially cut in order to accommodate them in the present volume. As the erotic content is the main point of interest here, material on astrology, charms, folk medicine and magic was the first to go. Further cuts were necessary and these were more subjective, ranging from Kalyana Malla's endless tables which seemed boring and impenetrable to Sheikh Nefzawi's racist or sexist stories which were judged offensive. Scholars will, of course, need to have complete texts including material on arbortifacients and the genitalia of animals, which have also been deleted – but this book is not intended for them.

The intention was to leave the original authors' essential erotic treatise supported by secondary material which gives background and colour, and where possible some feeling of the society in which the author was writing. The texts are as originally published in 1883 (Kama Sutra); 1885 (Ananga-Ranga) and 1886 (The Perfumed Garden). Only minor changes have been made (e.g. for consistency) in order to preserve the quality and tone of the Burton and Arbuthnot contribution. Often this has meant leaving very awkward constructions.

The original sequence has been retained except in the case of the Kama Sutra where – with the exception of the all important '64' which follows the order of Burton's Part II – considerable liberties were taken with reordering the other elements to make the abridged form more coherent. It is a pity that this change proved necessary particularly to the most important of the three books. However, Vatsyayana's work has survived worse indignities in the two millennia since it was written. Perhaps this editor – only the latest of a legion – can make amends to the old sage by quoting Richard Burton's beautiful eulogy:

'So long as lips shall kiss, and eyes shall see,
So long lives This, and This gives life to Thee.'

Illustrations

Although the miniature paintings which have been used to illustrate this book are part of a tradition which dates from the Muslim conquest of India, for religious reasons no corresponding school of painting exists in the Arab world. The illustrations which appear throughout the text of The Perfumed Garden – a product of the Arab culture of North Africa – are, therefore, designed to echo the mood of the writing, which is why predominantly Mughal paintings have been chosen, but they are importations.

Acknowledgement

It would not have been possible to illustrate this work so lavishly without the co-operation of two individuals.

Victor Lownes has generously provided several fine paintings from his splendid collection.

The editor would also like to acknowledge the very special contribution of Lance Dane. Lance's unrivalled understanding of Indian art, his encyclopedic knowledge of the numerous collections throughout the sub-continent, and his own fine collection, have been invaluable.

The painting of Sir Richard Burton is by kind permission of the National Portrait Gallery, London; the jacket subject is by courtesy of the Trustees of the Victoria and Albert Museum.

This edition first published in Great Britain in 1996 by Hamlyn, an imprint of Reed International Books Limited, Michelin House, 81 Fulham Road, London SW3 6RB

© Copyright Reed International Books Limited 1987

Reprinted 1998

ISBN 0 600 59097 6

A CIP catalogue record for this book is available from the British Library

Produced by Toppan Printing Co., (H.K.) Ltd.

Printed and bound in Hong Kong

CONTENTS

INTRODUCTION

The Relevance of a 2,000 year old Love Manual

At about the time that Saint John the Divine was agonizing over The Book of Revelation on the rocky island of Patmos in the Aegean, Vatsyayana, an elderly sage in the sacred city of Benares on the Ganges, was writing the Kama Sutra.

Both were men of religion: John, exiled by the emperor Domitian for his fiery evangelism, was concerned with prophecy and with instructing the seven Asian Churches of early Christianity; Vatsyayana, in the time-honoured custom of Hinduism, was ending his days as a religious student, composing his work 'according to the precepts of the Holy Writ'.

But the two ascetics could not have been more dissimilar. While John, the inspired poet, struggled to give form to apocalyptic visions from his own subconscious Vatsyayana, with quiet detachment, analysed the principles of sensual pleasure.

In Hinduism, sex is almost sacramental – essential to life and therefore worthy of serious study. Pleasures, said Vatsyayana are 'as necessary for the well-being of the body as food, are consequently equally required'. How different from the all-too-frequent association of sin and guilt with sex in the Judaeo-Christian tradition.

John's castigation, early in his Revelation, of the Church in Thyatira which seems to have relapsed into paganism, is full of sexual references. But more telling is his chosen metaphor for Rome, 'The Mother of Harlots and Abominations of the Earth . . . the woman was arrayed in purple and scarlet colour, and decked with gold and precious stones and pearls, having a golden cup in her hand full of abomination and filthiness of her fornication . . .'.[1] The tone is reminiscent of Ezekiel in the Old Testament: it is an image of women we find too often in Judaeo-Christian writing.[2]

Compare Vatsyayana's guiltless and frank description of his ideal 'Padmini' woman: 'Her eyes are bright and beautiful as the orb of the fawn. Her bosom is hard, full and high. Her yoni resembles the opening lotus bud,

and her love-seed is perfumed like the lily that has newly burst. She walks with a swan-like gait and her voice is low and musical. . . .'

It is not simply that John did not like women and Vatsyayana did (although that is obviously the case!): it is a fundamental difference between two cultures. So 'sinful' is sexual love, that the inclusion of the Song of Solomon, one of the world's greatest erotic poems, in the Bible had to be explained away with absurd comments to the effect that it is a metaphor for Christ's love of the Church.

The total absence of any sense of sexual guilt or sin is perhaps the most important message the modern reader in the West can receive from the Kama Sutra.[3]

Neurosis, unhappiness, or a prurient attitude to sex are not the only evils spawned by those who would have us believe that 'sin' and 'sex' are synonymous. The current of sexuality is too strong: those who would dam it, damn it indeed. The Marquis de Sade wrote: 'They have convinced me that through vice alone is man capable of experiencing this moral and physical vibration which is the source of the most delicious voluptuousness.'

Love is all you need?

The Kama Sutra is the most famous work on sex ever written. Although only the '64' – the second part of Sir Richard Burton's version – deals exclusively with sex, this is the 'Kama Sutra' of the popular imagination. There is much more to the work than that. Within the restraints of space, the other elements of the original which relate the 'sex-manual' to the society for which it was written have been retained.

The sexual content of the three works in this volume is the main purpose of the book, but sex is also the best bridge between those cultures and our own. Some anthropologists have been notorious for entering into the sexual lives of people they are studying in order to understand them better; Freud even connects the early sexual researches of children to the later development of their intellectual powers. Sex is a good way to begin understanding another culture, just as it is a good way to begin understanding another individual.

1. Readers of the King James Bible should always be grateful to the translator who, later in Revelation after The Woman on the Beast has perished, slipped in 'And the kings of the earth, who have committed fornication and lived *deliciously* with her, should bewail her . . .'

2. In early Buddhism the 'woman as temptress/vessel of iniquity' nonsense also had some currency before succumbing to the influence of Hinduism. The Arab Sheikh Nefzawi's 'Concerning the Tricks and Treacheries of Women' has been cut from the shortened version of 'The Perfumed Garden' included here.

3. The relevance of the Ananga-Ranga and The Perfumed Garden will be dealt with later.

The portrait of Sir Richard Burton by his friend Lord Leighton, first exhibited in 1875.

Rather less pompously: what could be more interesting than reading how people made love to each other in India at the time the Gospels were being written (Kama Sutra) or when Columbus was discovering the New World (Ananga-Ranga) or what instructed and titillated the Grand Vizier in Tunis while on the other side of the Mediterranean the Borgia Pope played illicit games with his daughter Lucrezia (The Perfumed Garden).

Richard Burton and his colleagues in the Kama Shastra Society published the Kama Sutra in 1883. But for more than half a century it was only a limited world of scholars, bibliophiles and gentlemen with a taste for the exotic retiring to their studies after dinner who knew of the existence of the classic. With the 1960s came popular knowledge of the Kama Sutra.

The most cursory look at contemporary newspaper headlines reminds us that the Sixties were not the dawn (or even the false dawn) of a golden age of tolerance. But the decade did see a powerful popular reaction to the deprivation and greyness of the post-war years. In its last great export, Liverpool – once the largest port in the world – re-worked and re-exported American music as it once had American cotton. The West had a new music-based culture centred on young people, their interests and preoccupations. A simultaneous explosion of hormones and spending power created an atmosphere in which the Kama Sutra could be openly published.

The book's Hindu origins at a time when everything Indian from Madras curry to yoga was fashionable – together with its famous 'positions' – placed the Kama Sutra firmly in the popular vocabulary and imagination.

Unfortunately it also joined the long list of unread classics. The Kama Sutra is generally regarded as a sex manual or worse still as pornography. Nothing could be less pornographic, but nor should it be treated as a step-by-step love manual. Many of the asanas – or love-making positions – are only possible for yoga adepts or, at least, very supple athletes. The cook-book approach to love-making (another creation of the Sixties) which made much of 'foreplay' and fixed the always mispronounced clitoris in the male imagination as a kind of go-button[4] – has nothing to do with the Kama Sutra.

Kama Sutra, Ananga-Ranga and The Perfumed Garden

The Kama Sutra is the most important of the three works included in this book; it is also the oldest. The author, whose full name was Mallinaga Vatsyayana, was compiler as much as author. His sources were the vast body of Hindu erotology which already existed by the first century A.D., although even in the Burton/ Arbuthnot version, with its many infelicities of style,

4. Ironically it means 'shutter'.

the personality of the old sage is stamped on his work.

A 'sutra' is an aphorism, the briefest possible statement of a principle. The sutra was probably favoured because writing was not widespread during this period and students could memorize important texts more easily. All the important Sanskrit works on logic, grammar and philosophy were written in sutras.

Having been condensed in this way, the ideas needed the 'rehydration' of commentary to render them comprehensible, and the tenth century Jayamangala commentary was that mainly used by Burton's pandits. Miraculously, something of Vatsyayana, the man himself, survived all this. Worldly-wise but not world-weary, he approaches his subject with a detachment that is sometimes almost clinical. Yet it is a human book above all else, a masterpiece of tolerance and good sense. Although 'some learned men object' Vatsyayana insists that women should read his work: he argues the case with his usual blend of pragmatism and humanity.

All later Indian writers could only follow the old sage, and indeed through the centuries the least among them acknowledge the fact. In the Kama Sutra, Vatsyayana wrote one of the great books of the world.

The Ananga-Ranga or Stage of the Bodiless One is a creation of the Indian Middle Ages. How different life had become since Vatsyayana's time! In ancient India there was no seclusion of women, and pre-marital and extra-marital sex were evidently common. Kalyana Malla, author of the Anaga-Ranga, lived in a rigid and strict society where child marriage was common and unattached men and women had few opportunities to meet.

If society abounded in rules so does the Ananga-Ranga. The positive rules are bewildering in their detail: 'at the time of the new moon the Hastini woman's yoni should be manipulated and pulled open like a flower.' There are similar detailed instructions on what to do to which part (including the big toe) of each type of woman during the eight watches of the day and night throughout the entire lunar calendar. And woe betide anyone who made a mistake!

The negative rules are equally daunting. Kalyana Malla lists prohibitions on what not to do, where not to do it and with whom not to consider doing it, in a tone occasionally bordering on the hysterical.

Although a pedant, with a very high opinion of himself, Kalyana Malla sets himself the praiseworthy task of ensuring that the rigidity of contemporary marriage did not become boring to either partner. And despite the many irrelevant accretions (astrology, palmistry etc.) he gives a great deal of useful and well-considered advice. Some of the sexual advice is superior to Vatsyayana's. The principal difference between the two is that Vatsyayana was writing for lovers – Kalyana Malla's readership were husbands. Although an inferior work compared with the Kama Sutra, it could be argued that the Ananga-Ranga – with its stated intention of ensuring that one sexual partner is enough for anyone – has greater relevance for a society plagued by the AIDS virus.

All three erotic texts in this book were written by men. That each author was the product of his society, writing from the point of view of his gender, is of course a truism: it is these differences of approach and content which make the inclusion of the three famous love manuals published by The Kama Shastra Society a valuable exercise. But Vatsyayana and Kalyana Malla were men writing for men and women: Sheikh Nefzawi was a man writing for men – and he was a rather dirty old man at that. He was also more of a poet than the other two put together. Sheikh Nefzawi also had humour, something sadly lacking in most erotology. Although he would have sneered at the cuts that have been made to his work here, he has suffered no greater abbreviation than the other authors. And the Burton translation is in itself incomplete, as will be explained at the end of this introduction.

Although fourteen centuries separate the Ananga-Ranga and the Kama Sutra, they are part of the same cultural heritage: the similarities between the two worlds in which they were written are as striking as the differences. India's ability to assimilate the cultures of different invaders (and by the period of the Ananga-Ranga Islam held sway in the sub-continent) is remarkable – somehow each new influence was gradually absorbed to become part of what is India. The Perfumed Garden came from a very different culture indeed.

The Tunis in which Sheikh Nefzawi wrote The Perfumed Garden was balanced precariously between Spain's appetite for new conquests in North Africa, the fragile independence of a few Muslim states, and the unstoppable janissaries of the Ottoman Empire. After Pope Alexander Borgia was bribed to poison the Sultan's brother, the Turks under the leadership of Beyezid, Selim and then Suleiman 'The Magnificent', conquered Persia and Egypt and even made incursions into Europe as far as Ratisbon in Germany.

Contemporary Tunis was famed for its mosques, scholars and encouragement of learning. In this rich and luxurious city Sheikh Nefzawi would have had little trouble in finding a ready patron for his own particular branch of letters. It was a typical device in Arab literature to elaborate and dramatize a point by telling a story, thus creating a kind of secular parable. Burton would have certainly translated these pieces himself. The translator's enthusiasm all helps to confirm Sheikh Nefzawi's place as a master of salacious writing; a minor star in a firmament which includes Boccaccio and John Cleland – and of course Burton himself.

Sir Richard Burton and The Kama Shastra Society (London and Benares)

To attempt to get Richard Burton into a few pages of introduction is rather like pursuing a gigantic, malevolent djinn with an empty bottle. An improbable array of writers have tried to capture Burton: his piously Catholic and devoted wife Isabel; his Protestant and rather prickly niece Georgiana Stisted; wily old Frank Harris and a host of others, right up to the present. Somehow, none ever quite got the cork in the neck of the bottle: the djinn's laughter mocks them all!

The physical appearance of Richard Burton is a good place to begin. Not only was it remarkable in itself, it gives some idea of the effect the man had on people. There are many portraits which speak for themselves but the first-hand descriptions are also interesting. The traveller and poet Wilfrid Blunt wrote:

'His dress and appearance were those suggesting a released convict rather than anything of more repute. He reminded me by turns of a black leopard, caged but unforgiving, and again with his close-cut pol and iron frame, of that wonderful creation of Balzac's, the ex-galérien Vautrin, hiding his grim identity under an Abbé's cassock. He wore, habitually, a rusty black coat with a crumpled black silk stock, his throat destitute of collar, a costume which his muscular frame and immense chest made singularly and incongruously hideous, above it a countenance the most sinister I have ever seen, dark, cruel, treacherous, with eyes like a wild beast's. . . .' The critic Arthur Symons spoke of a 'mouth that aches with desire, with those dilated nostrils that drink in I know not what strange perfumes.'[5]

Blunt and Symons are describing the man in his forties when his experience of the world and some physical scarring had touched Burton with a satanic glamour. But genes had their part to play as well, and in his father Lieutenant-Colonel Joseph Burton were the makings of his own striking physiognomy. Richard Burton said of him: 'Although of very mixed blood, he was more a Roman in appearance than anything else, of moderate height, dark hair, sallow skin, high nose and piercing black eyes.'

It was not only the 'piercing black eyes' of his Anglo-Irish father than he inherited. There was also a recklessness and restlessness in Joseph that propelled the family endlessly from home to home throughout Europe. The son was also to become a wanderer.

Richard may have been in the same mould, with some of the same characteristics, as his father but the substance

5. Contemporary novels created several unforgettable characters which often seem to have something of Burton in them – or was it that he had something of them? It was as if Byron's personality had fragmented, but lived on in Heathcliff (1842), Rochester (1842) and some of Edward Bulwer-Lytton's and Benjamin Disraeli's characters.

of the man was very different. His restlessness included his intellect. Ensuring his early rustication from Oxford by duelling and refusing to conform, he joined the Bombay Native Infantry at Baroda in 1842. Disliked by most of his fellow officers, and happier in the company of his Hindu 'bubu' girl who shared his bungalow, Burton became known as the 'white nigger'.

It was not his domestic arrangements which earned him the name (these were quite usual) but his passion for the East, its culture and its languages.[6] There was also his predilection for dressing as a native and using his fluency in the different Indian languages to pass undetected through the bazaar at night. It was this facility which encouraged his commander, Sir Charles Napier, to use Burton as a spy. It was a role which suited the young ensign's personality as well as his talents: it was secret and dangerous, it brought him close to the throbbing intimate pulse of life, it was something only he could do. But as so often with Burton, the brilliance which dazzled others burned its author. He achieved so much, enough to fill a dozen lives, but time and time again when everything seemed to be going his way, he was cast down. Cast down not by fate but by the demons in his own personality.

In Karachi, Burton was asked by Napier to report on the brothels frequented by the army. Bordellos were regarded as a necessary evil in a garrison town, but syphilis impaired efficiency and Napier wanted a survey. He got more than he bargained for! The General, who was noted for his ruthlessness in action, was deeply shocked to learn that three of the brothels catered for homosexuals. His naïveté must have surprised Burton, but the ensign was dispatched to prepare a comprehensive confidential report in order that the luparnars might be closed. The report could not have been more comprehensive or, ultimately, less confidential.

Richard Burton had already met the doctor and orientalist John Steinhaeuser who shared his interest in exotic erotology. Perhaps is was this shared passion for the bizarre[7] which prompted him to fill the report with so much detail on the practices of the eunuchs and the boys, and the demands made by clients. Perhaps it was.

The army had never been the right place for Richard Burton. The army knew it and he knew it – and now the army thought it knew something else about him. A further three years in India were enough. In 1849, depressed and ill, he left for England.

From 1850 onwards, until his death in 1890, most of what we know of Richard Burton has passed through the efficient purification filter of his wife, Isabel. The early

part of her 'life' of her husband is based on his account. From 1850 onwards we see him almost entirely through her eyes. It was in that year they met in Boulogne, although they did not marry until 1860. At her first sight of him, striding along the ramparts, she declared to her sister 'that man will marry me'.

There is an inevitability about everything to do with Richard Burton. Much has been written on the unsuitability of his marriage to Isabel, but that too was, it seems, pre-ordained. It is a matter of record that before leaving for Boulogne Isabel had her fortune told by a Romany called Hagar Burton: 'You will cross the sea, and be in the same town with your Destiny, and know it not. Every obstacle will rise up against you, and such a combination of circumstances, that it will require all your courage and energy and intelligence to meet them. Your life will be like one always swimming against big waves, but God will always be with you, so you will always win. You will fix your eye on your polar star, and you will go for that without looking right or left. You will bear the name of our Tribe, and be right proud of it. You will be as we are, but far greater than we. Your life is all wandering, change, and adventure. One soul in two bodies, in life or death; never long apart. Show this to the man you take for your husband.'

The gypsy's horoscope could not have been more accurate: she had the gift of second sight and glimpsed part of the pattern of his life. Researching Burton one is struck forcibly by the idea that the entire pattern was always there, like an eastern carpet with the same motif repeated.

In the decade that followed he made two of the greatest achievements of his life and those which brought him fame. In 1853, disguised as a Pathan, Richard Burton made the pilgrimage to Mecca. He was not the first unbeliever audacious enough to take the terrible risk, but his account of his experiences (Pilgrimage to Al-Medinah and Meccah, 1855) is a marvellous creation.

Then began the period of African exploration, culminating in the most famous of all his journeys: the trip undertaken with John Speke to search for the source of the Nile. After suffering terrible hardships, Speke and Burton discovered Lake Tanganyika. This vast inland sea was sure to be the source of the Nile, and after a hasty survey they returned to the town of Kazeh. Here they rested and prepared for the return journey to the coast. Speke wanted to explore further to the north before returning; there was rumoured to be a further lake. Burton refused and Speke was obliged to go alone. The pattern repeated itself: with complete success in his grasp, Richard Burton let it slip away. It was Speke and not Burton who discovered Lake Victoria, the true source of the Nile.

This was not the last time the pattern would repeat. Years later, when the bitter acrimony which followed the

---

6. At his death Burton was fluent in at least forty languages.
7. Steinhaeuser remained a friend throughout his life and was the first with whom Richard Burton could share his scholarly interest in exotic subjects of all kinds. He did not meet F.F. Arbuthnot, who was twelve years his junior, until 1853.

*As they have for centuries, trading feluccas moor for the night on the banks of the Nile.
Burton's search for the source of the great river was the zenith of his career as an explorer.*

Nile expedition and Speke's mysterious death were distant memories, and after a series of inappropriate Foreign Office appointments, he was made Consul of Damascus. Now approaching fifty and not well, it was the perfect final appointment for a passionate Arabist and a kind gesture on the part of Lord Clarendon. Mismanaging a wonderful opportunity, he was removed to Trieste where, eighteen years later, he was to die.

The gypsy had not exaggerated: a life of 'swimming against big waves.' Through every difficulty Isabel supported her increasingly irascible and cantankerous husband. At Trieste his study came to embrace the world. In a large room several tables, each covered with all the work relating to a particular book, were arrayed, so that Burton could move from one to another as the mood took him, as once he had moved from country to country.

If they thought they had contained him he would soon prove them wrong. If they thought the exploration was at an end they were fools. The secrets of the Arabian Nights were there waiting to be discovered, there were hidden places in Hindu literature too, and he alone had a key to the scented garden. . . .

The door of Burton's study was metaphorically, and on occasions literally, closed to Isabel. The devoutly religious and conventional woman was not interested to know that 'pomegranite' is a name for anus among the Arabs or that infibulation was practised by this tribe or that. There were men who were deeply interested in such exotica, however, and these were the members of the Kama Shastra Society.

The Kama Shastra Society is almost as elusive as its creator. The false clues and blind alleys which surround it were not simply a reflection of Burton's love of mystery, they were a very necessary protection for an enterprise whose intention was to publish erotica.

A vast book-buying public existed in the late Victorian period, of which a significant proportion were eager consumers of 'exotica'. Publishers and printers in London, Paris and Amsterdam produced material for every level of readership, from trash and the worst kind of pornography to erotic literature and serious scholarly works. The great collector and bibliographer of this, and earlier, material was Henry Ashbee, who was one of those involved with the Society.[8] The print farmer, and friend of Aubrey Beardsley, Leonard Smithers, was also an associate and on the periphery were Richard Monckton Milnes (Lord Houghton) and Algernon Swinburne. But the joint founder of the Kama Shastra Society of London and Benares[9] and co-author with Burton of several of its important works was Foster Arbuthnot.

In the glamour which has always surrounded Richard Burton, the contribution of Foster Arbuthnot has been rather neglected. Although Isabel did not approve of their literary collaboration, she understood the strength of the bond between the two men: when Richard died she gave a gold chain to Arbuthnot as a keepsake for 'his best friend'. How the two worked together is not clear, although Arbuthnot regarded himself as a collector of facts rather than a writer, and probably produced a rough draft from the first translation which Burton then polished and annotated in his own unique way. The curious collaboration between the gentle, sensitive Arbuthnot and Burton was both an artistic and a financial success.

On Sunday 19th October, 1890, Isabel returned from Mass to find Richard working on the last page of The Perfumed Garden. It was, although she did not then know it, a new translation of a whole section omitted from the original Kama Shastra Society version – it dealt with homosexuality and pederasty. Burton's health had been in rapid decline for some time: a doctor lived permanently with them in the house at Trieste. Two days earlier he had told Isabel that a bird had tapped on his window and told her 'that bird is a bad omen you know.' She had refused to accept it as such, reminding him that the birds were used to him feeding them from his window-sill. Richard replied enigmatically: 'Ah, it was not that window, but another.'

It was the completion of the pattern, he knew he was dying. It must have given him great pleasure that this time there would be no slipping of the cup from his lip, he would not be cheated at the end. He had finished work on the all important new section of The Perfumed Garden. The final touches to the work were made on the Sunday. He died before dawn the next day.

When Isabel read the manuscript she feared dreadfully for the reputation of her husband, her beloved Jemmy. She consigned it, more than a thousand pages, to the fire.

8. Ashbee awarded himself the scatological pseudonym 'Pisanus Fraxi'. He is thought by some to be the real 'Walter' – author of the notorious autobiography – but somehow lacks the right qualities to be that old rascal.
9. More obfuscation: in this case the fog which hung about the reservoirs of Stoke Newington where Smithers had found a 'safe' printer. Miraculously Stoke Newington became the ancient city of Benares.

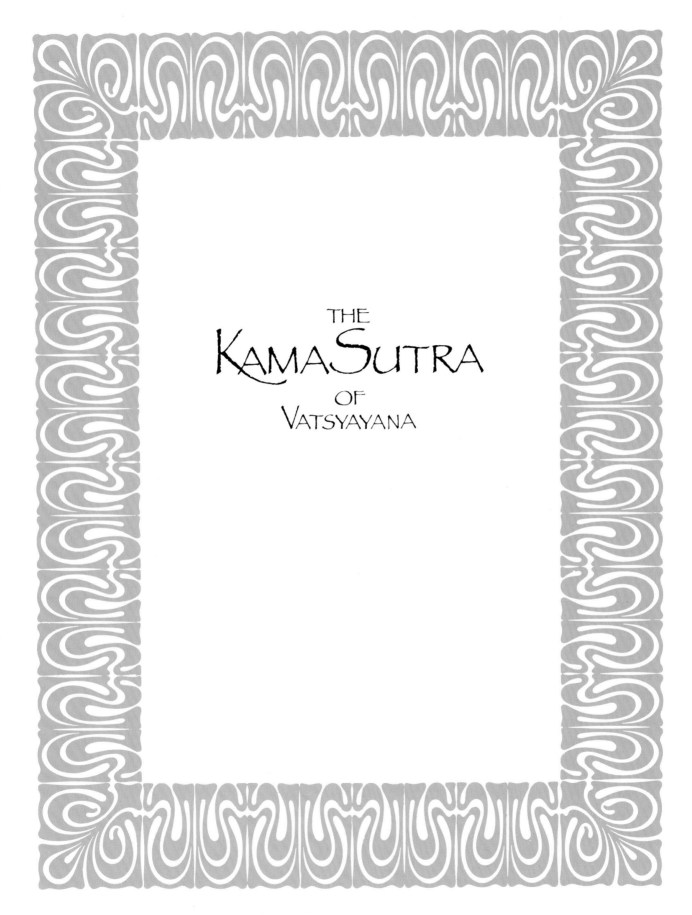

THE
KAMA SUTRA
OF
VATSYAYANA

The Acquisition of Dharma, Artha and Kama

Man, the period of whose life is one hundred years, should practise Dharma, Artha and Kama at different times and in such a manner that they may harmonize together and not clash in any way. He should acquire learning in his childhood, in his youth and in his middle age he should attend to Artha and Kama, and in his old age he should perform Dharma, and thus seek to gain Moksha, the release from further transmigration. Or, on account of the uncertainty of life, he may practise them at times when they are enjoined to be practised. But one thing is to be noted, he should lead the life of a religious student until he finishes his education.

Dharma is obedience to the command of the Shastra or Holy Writ of the Hindus to do certain things, such as the performance of sacrifices, which are not generally done, because they do not belong to this world, and produce no visible effect; and not to do other things, such as eating meat, which is often done because it belongs to this world, and has visible effects.

Dharma should be learnt from the Shruti (Holy Writ), and from those conversant with it.

Artha is the acquisition of arts, land, gold, cattle, wealth, equipages and friends. It is, further, the protection of what is acquired, and the increase of what is protected.

Artha should be learnt from the king's officers, and from merchants who may be versed in the ways of commerce.

Kama is the enjoyment of appropriate objects by the five senses of hearing, feeling, seeing, tasting and smelling, assisted by the mind together with the soul. The ingredient in this is a peculiar contact between the organ of sense and its object, and the consciousness of pleasure which arises from that contact is called Kama.

Kama is to be learnt from the Kama Sutra (aphorisms on love) and from the practice of citizens.

Thus I have written in a few words the 'Science of love', after reading the texts of ancient authors, and following the ways of enjoyment mentioned in them.

He who is acquainted with the true principles of this science pays regard to Dharma, Artha, Kama and to his own experiences, as well as to the teachings of others and does not act simply on the dictates of his own desire. As for the errors in the science of love which I have mentioned in this work, on my own authority as an author, I have, immediately after mentioning them, carefully censured and prohibited them.

An act is never looked upon with indulgence for the simple reason that it is authorized by the science, because it ought to be remembered that it is the intention of the science, that the rules which it contains should only be acted upon in particular cases. After reading and considering the works of Babhravya and other ancient authors, and thinking over the meaning of the rules given by them, the Kama Sutra was composed, according to the precepts of Holy Writ, for the benefit of the world, by Vatsyayana, while leading the life of a religious student, and wholly engaged in the contemplation of the Deity.

This work is not intended to be used merely as an instrument for satisfying our desires. A person, acquainted with the true principles of this science, and who preserves his Dharma, Artha, and Kama, and has regard for the practices of the people, is sure to obtain the mastery over his senses.

In short, an intelligent and prudent person, attending to Dharma and Artha, and attending to Kama also, without becoming the slave of his passions, obtains success in everything that he may undertake.

The Arts and Sciences to be Studied

1. The bewildering list of 'arts' has been omitted for reasons of length, but ranges from making artificial flowers and playing on musical glasses filled with water, to knowledge of mines and quarries, and warfare.

Man should study the Kama Sutra and the arts and sciences[1] subordinate thereto, in addition to the study of the arts and sciences contained in Dharma and Artha. Even young maids should study this Kama Sutra along with its arts and sciences before marriage, and after it they should continue to do so with the consent of their husbands.

Here some learned men object, and say that females, not being allowed to study any science, should not study the Kama Sutra. But Vatsyayana is of opinion that this objection does not hold good. If a wife becomes separated from her husband, and falls into distress, she can support herself easily, even in a foreign country, by means of her knowledge of these arts. Even the bare knowledge of them gives attractiveness to a woman, although the practice of them may be only possible or otherwise according to the circumstances of each case. A man who is versed in these arts, who is loquacious and acquainted with the arts of gallantry, gains very soon the hearts of women, even though he is only acquainted with them for a short time.

Traditional postures of the kind only to be enjoyed by yoga adepts (Grissa style, Bengal).

The Life of a Citizen

Having thus acquired learning, a man, with the wealth that he may have gained by gift, conquest, purchase, deposit[2] or inheritance from his ancestors, should become a householder and pass the life of a citizen. He should take a house in a city, or large village, or in the vicinity of good men, or in a place which is the resort of many persons. This abode should be situated near some water, and divided into different compartments for different purposes. It should be surrounded by a garden, and also contain two rooms, an outer and an inner one. The inner room should be occupied by the females, while the outer room, balmy with rich perfumes, should contain a bed, soft, agreeable to the sight, covered with a clean white cloth, low in the middle part, having garlands and bunches of flowers upon it, and a canopy above it, and two pillows, one at the top, another at the bottom. There should be also a sort of couch besides and at the head of this a sort of stool, on which should be placed the fragrant ointments for the night, as well as flowers, pots containing collyrium and other fragrant substances, things used for perfuming the mouth, and the bark of the common citron tree. Near the couch, on the ground, there should be a pot for spitting, a box containing ornaments, and also a lute hanging from a peg made of the tooth of an elephant, a board for drawing, a pot containing perfume, some books, and some garlands of the yellow amaranth flowers. Not far from the couch and on the ground, there should be a round seat, a toy cart, and a board for playing with dice; outside the outer room there should be cases of birds and a separate place for spinning, carving and such like diversions. In the garden there should be a whirling swing and a common swing, as also a bower of creepers covered with flowers, in which a raised parterre should be made for sitting.

Now the householder, having got up in the morning and performed his necessary duties, should wash his teeth, apply a limited quantity of ointments and perfumes to his body, put some ornaments on his person and collyrium on his eyelids and below his eyes, colour his lips with alacktaka, and look at himself in the glass. Having then eaten betel leaves, with other things that give fragrance to the mouth, he should perform his usual business. He should bathe daily, anoint his body with oil every other day, apply a lathering substance to his body every three days, get his head (including face) shaved every four days, and the other parts of his body every five or ten days. All these things should be done without fail, and the sweat of the armpits should also be removed. Meals should be taken in the forenoon, in the afternoon and again at night, according to Charayana. After breakfast, parrots and other birds should be taught to speak, and the fighting of cocks, quails, and rams should follow. A limited time should be devoted to diversions with Pitharmardas, Vitas and Vidushakas* and then should be taken the midday sleep. After this the householder, having put on his clothes and ornaments, should, during the afternoon, converse with his friends. In the evening there should be singing, and after that the householder, along with his friend, should await in his room, previously decorated and perfumed, the arrival of the woman that may be attached to him, or he may send a female messenger for her, or go to her himself. After her arrival at his house, he and his friend should welcome her, and entertain her with a loving and agreeable conversation. Thus end the duties of the day.

The following are the things to be done occasionally as diversions or amusements.

Holding festivals in honour of different Deities
Social gatherings of both sexes
Drinking parties

Picnics
Other social diversions

2. Acquiring possessions by gift is peculiar to Brahmans, the priestly caste; conquest is associated with the warrior kshatryas, and other methods with the Vaishyas or mercantile caste.

*See footnote 21, page 66

Marriage

When Kama is practised by men of the four castes according to the rules of the Holy Writ (i.e. by lawful marriage) with virgins of their own caste, it then becomes a means of acquiring lawful progeny and good fame.

When a girl becomes marriageable her parents should dress her smartly, and should place her where she can be easily seen by all. Every afternoon, having dressed her and decorated her in a becoming manner, they should send her with her female companions to sports, sacrifices, and marriage ceremonies, and thus show her to advantage in society. They should also receive with kind words and signs of friendliness those of an auspicious appearance who may come accompanied by their friends and relations for the purpose of marrying their daughter, and under some pretext or other having first dressed her becomingly, should then present her to them. After this they should await the pleasure of fortune, and with this object should appoint a future day on which a determination could be come to with regard to their daughter's marriage. On this occasion, when the persons have come, the parents of the girl should ask them to bathe and dine, and should say, 'Everything will take place at the proper time', and should not then comply with the request but should settle the matter later.

Regular depilation was considered essential for fastidious lovers (Deccan).

Although Vatsyayana counsels his reader to act according to his own inclination, he felt that fellatio was generally practised only by 'unchaste and wanton women.'

When a girl is thus acquired either according to the custom of the country, or according to his own desire, the man should marry her in accordance with the precepts of the Holy Writ, according to one of the four kinds of marriage.[3]

Amusement in society, such as completing verses begun by others, marriage, and auspicious ceremonies should be carried on neither with superiors, nor inferiors, but with our equals. That should be known as a high connection when a man, after marrying a girl, has to serve her and her relations afterwards like a servant, and such a connection is censured by the good. On the other hand, that reproachable connection, where a man together with his relations, lords it over his wife, is called a low connection by the wise. But when both the man and the woman afford mutual pleasure to each other, and where the relatives on both sides pay respect to one another, such is called a connection in the proper sense of the word. Therefore a man should contract neither a high connection by which he is obliged to bow down afterwards to his kinsmen, nor a low connection, which is universally reprehended by all. A girl who is much sought after should marry the man that she likes, and whom she thinks would be obedient to her, and capable of giving her pleasure. But when from the desire of wealth a girl is married by her parents to a rich man without taking into consideration the character or looks of the bridegroom, or when given to a man who has several wives, she never becomes attached to the man, even though he be endowed with good qualities, obedient to her will, active, strong, and healthy and anxious to please her in every way. A husband who is obedient but yet master of himself, though he be poor and not good looking, is better than one who is common to many women, even though he be handsome and attractive. The wives of rich men, where there are many wives, are not generally attached to their husbands, and are not confidential with them, and even though they possess all the external enjoyments of life, still have recourse to other men. A man who is of a low mind, who has fallen from his social position, and who is much given to travelling, does not deserve to be married; neither does one who has many wives and children, or one who is devoted to sport and gambling and who comes to his wife only when he likes. Of all the lovers of a girl he only is her true husband who possesses the qualities that are liked by her, and such a husband only enjoys real superiority over her, because he is the husband of love.

Creating Confidence in the Girl

For the first three days after marriage, the girl and her husband should sleep on the floor, abstain from sexual pleasures, and eat their food without seasoning it either with alkali or salt. For the next seven days they should bathe amidst the sounds of auspicious musical instruments, should decorate themselves, dine together, and pay attention to their relations as well as to those who may have come to witness their marriage. This is applicable to persons of all castes. On the night of the tenth day the man should begin in a lonely place with soft words, and thus create confidence in the girl. Some authors say that for the purpose of winning her over he should not speak to her for three days, but the followers of Babhravya are of opinion that if the man does not speak with her for three days, the girl may be discouraged by seeing him spiritless like a pillar, and, becoming dejected, she may begin to despise him as an eunuch. Vatsyayana says that the man should begin to win her over, and to create confidence in her, but should abstain at first from sexual pleasures. Women being of a tender nature, want tender beginnings, and when they are forcibly approached by men with

3. It should be remembered that polygamy was normal.

*Study of love-texts was essential if a rich man with many
wives was to keep them all satisfied (Rajasthan).*

whom they are but slightly acquainted, they sometimes suddenly become haters of sexual connection, and sometimes even haters of the male sex. The man should therefore approach the girl according to her liking, and should make use of those devices by which he may be able to establish himself more and more into her confidence. These devices are as follows:—

He should embrace her first of all in the way she likes most, because it does not last for a long time.

He should embrace her with the upper part of his body, because that is easier and simpler. If the girl is grown up, or if the man has known her for some time, he may embrace her by the light of a lamp, but if he is not well acquainted with her, or if she is a young girl, he should then embrace her in darkness.

When the girl accepts the embrace, the man should put a 'tambula' or screw of betel nut and betel leaves in her mouth, and if she will not take it, he should induce her to do so by conciliatory words, entreaties, oaths, and kneeling at her feet, for it is a universal rule that however bashful or angry a woman may be, she never disregards a man's kneeling at her feet. At the time of giving this 'tambula' he should kiss her mouth softly and gracefully without making any sound. When she is gained over in this respect he should then make her talk, and so that she may be induced to talk he should ask her questions about things of which he knows or pretends to know nothing, and which can be answered in a few words. If she does not speak to him, he should not frighten her, but should ask her the same thing again and again in a conciliatory manner. If she does not then speak he should urge her to give a reply, because as Ghotakamukha says, 'all girls hear everything said to them by men, but do not themselves sometimes say a single word.' When she is thus importuned, the girl should give replies by shakes of the head, but if she has quarrelled with the man she should not even do that. When she is asked by the man whether she wishes for him, and whether she likes him, she should remain silent for a long time, and when at last importuned to reply, should give him a favourable answer by a nod of her head. If the man is previously acquainted with the girl he should converse with her by means of a female friend, who may be favourable to him, and in the confidence of both, and carry on the conversation on both sides. On such an occasion the girl should smile with her head bent down, and if the female friend says more on her part than she was desired to do, she should chide her and dispute with her. The female friend should say in jest even what she is not desired to say by the girl, and add, 'she says so,' on which the girl should say indistinctly and prettily, 'Oh no! I did not say so,' and she should then smile and throw an occasional glance towards the man.

If the girl is familiar with the man, she should place near him, without saying anything, the tambula, the ointment, or the garland that he may have asked for, or she may tie them up in his upper garment. While she is engaged in this, the man should touch her young breasts in the sounding way of pressing with the nails, and if she prevents him doing this he should say to her, 'I will not do it again if you will embrace me,' and should in this way cause her to embrace him. While he is being embraced by her he should pass his hand repeatedly over and about her body. By and by he should place her in his lap, and try more and more to gain her consent, and if she will not yield to him he should frighten her by saying 'I shall impress marks of my teeth and nails on your lips and breasts, and then make similar marks on my own body, and shall tell my friends that you did them. What will you say then?' In this and other ways, as fear and confidence are created in the minds of children, so should the man gain her over to his wishes.

On the second and third nights, after her confidence has increased still more, he should feel the whole of her body with his hands, and kiss her all over; he should also

The sage Suvarnanabha advises that during lovemaking a man should press those parts
of the woman's body on which she turns her eyes (Rajasthan).

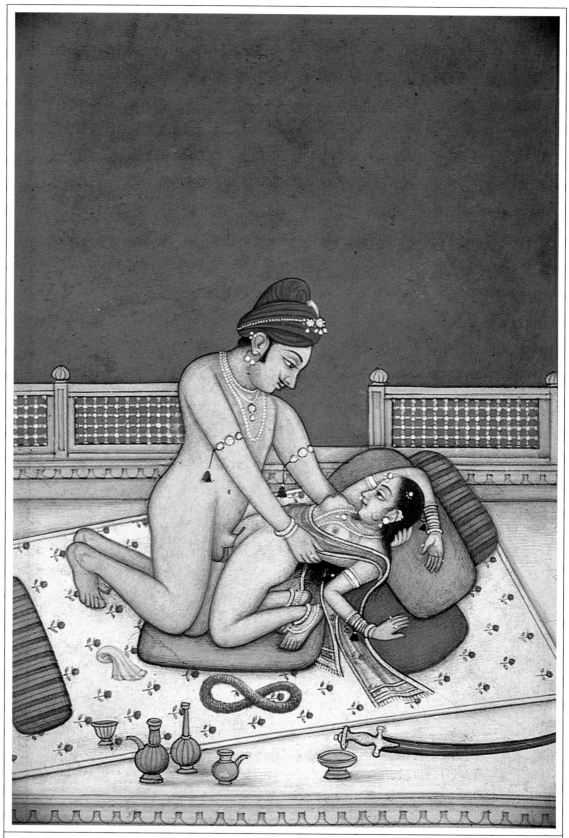

Imagination in lovemaking generates 'love, friendship, and respect in the hearts of women' (Rajasthan).

place his hands upon her thighs and shampoo them, and if he succeeds in this he should then shampoo the joints of her thighs. If she tries to prevent him doing this he should say to her, 'What harm is there in doing it?' and should persuade her to let him do it. After gaining this point he should touch her private parts, should loosen her girdle and the knot of her dress, and turning up her lower garment should shampoo the joints of her naked thighs. Under various pretences he should do all these things, but he should not at that time begin actual congress. After this he should teach her the sixty-four arts, should tell her how much he loves her, and describe to her the hopes which he formerly entertained regarding her. He should also promise to be faithful to her in future and should dispel all her fears with respect to rival women, and, at last, after having overcome her bashfulness, he should begin to enjoy her in a way so as not to frighten her. So much about creating a confidence in the girl; and there are moreover, some verses on the subject as follows:

A man acting according to the inclinations of a girl should try and gain her over so that she may love him and place her confidence in him. A man does not succeed either by implicitly following the inclination of a girl, or by wholly opposing her, and he should therefore adopt a middle course. He who knows how to make himself beloved by women, as well as to increase their honour and create confidence in them, this man becomes an object of their love. But he who neglects a girl thinking she is too bashful, is despised by her as a beast ignorant of the working of the female mind. Moreover, a girl forcibly enjoyed by one who does not understand the hearts of girls becomes nervous, uneasy, and dejected, and suddenly begins to hate the man who has taken advantage of her; and then, when her love is not understood or returned, she sinks into despondency, and becomes either a hater of mankind altogether, or, hating her own man, she has recourse to other men.

The Virtuous Wife

A virtuous woman, who has affection for her husband, should act in conformity with his wishes as if he were a divine being, and with his consent should take upon herself the whole care of his family. She should keep the whole house well cleaned, and arrange flowers of various kinds in different parts of it, and make the floor smooth and polished so as to give the whole a neat and becoming appearance. She should surround the house with a garden, and place ready in it all the materials required for the morning, noon and evening sacrifices.

The wife, whether she be a woman of noble family, or a virgin widow[4] remarried, or a concubine, should lead a chaste life, devoted to her husband, and doing everything for his welfare. Women acting thus, acquire Dharma, Artha, and Kama, obtain a high position, and generally keep their husbands devoted to them.

4. This probably refers to a girl married in her infancy, or when very young, and whose husband had died before she arrived at the age of puberty. (Burton)

The Wives of Other Men

The wives of other people may be resorted to but it must be distinctly understood that it is only allowed for special reasons and not for mere carnal desire.[5] The possibility of their acquisition, their fitness for cohabitation, the danger to oneself in uniting with

5. Numerous acceptable reasons for adultery are listed by Vatsyayana with icy objectivity. They include when a man thinks 'by being united with this woman, I shall kill her husband, and so obtain his vast riches which I covet' and 'the husband of this woman has violated the chastity of my wives, I shall therefore return that injury by seducing his wives.'

them, and the future effect of these unions, should first of all be examined. A man may resort to the wife of another, for the purpose of saving his own life, when he perceives that his love for her proceeds from one degree of intensity to another. These degrees are ten in number, and are distinguished by the following marks:–

1. Love of the eye
2. Attachment of the mind
3. Constant reflection
4. Destruction of sleep
5. Emaciation of the body
6. Turning away from objects of enjoyment
7. Removal of shame
8. Madness
9. Fainting
10. Death

The causes of a woman rejecting the addresses of a man are as follows:–

1. Affection for her husband
2. Desire of lawful progeny
3. Want of opportunity
4. Anger at being addressed by the man too familiarly
5. Difference in rank of life
6. Want of certainty on account of the man being devoted to travelling
7. Thinking that the man may be attached to some other person
8. Fear of the man's not keeping his intentions secret
9. Thinking that the man is too devoted to his friends, and has too great a regard for them
10. The apprehension that he is not in earnest
11. Bashfulness on account of his being an illustrious man
12. Fear on account of his being powerful, or possessed of too impetuous passion, in the case of the 'deer' woman
13. Bashfulness on account of his being too clever
14. The thought of having once lived with him on friendly terms only
15. Contempt of his want of knowledge of the world
16. Distrust of his low character
17. Disgust at his want of perception of her love for him
18. In the case of an 'elephant' woman, the thought that he is a 'hare' man, or a man weak of passion
19. Compassion lest anything should befall him on account of his passion
20. Despair at her own imperfections
21. Fear of discovery
22. Disillusion at seeing his grey hair or shabby appearance
23. Fear that he may be employed by her husband to test her chastity
24. The thought that he has too much regard for morality

The Women of the Royal Harem and of the Keeping of One's Own Wife

The women of the royal harem cannot see or meet any men on account of their being strictly guarded, neither do they give pleasure to each other in various ways as now described.

Having dressed the daughters of their nurses, or their female friends, or their female attendants, like men, they accomplish their object by means of bulbs, roots, and fruits having the form of the lingam, or they lie down upon the statue of a male figure, in which the lingam is visible and erect.

'Of all the lovers of a girl he only is her true husband who possesses the qualities that are liked by her . . . because he is the husband of love' (Rajasthan).

Some Kings, who are compassionate, take or apply certain medicines to enable them to enjoy many wives in one night, simply for the purpose of satisfying the desire of their women, though they perhaps have no desire of their own. Others enjoy with great affection only those wives that they particularly like, while others only take them, according as the turn of each wife arrives, in due course.

By means of their female attendants the ladies of the royal harem generally get men into their apartments in the disguise or dress of women. Their female attendants and the daughters of their nurses, who are acquainted with their secrets, should exert themselves to get men to come to the harem in this way by telling them of the good fortune attending it, and by describing the facilities of entering and leaving the palace, the large size of the premises, the carelessness of the sentinels, and the irregularities of the attendants about the persons of the royal wives. But these women should never induce a man to enter the harem by telling him falsehoods, for that would probably lead to his destruction.

The entrance of young men into harems, and their exits from them, generally take place when things are being brought into the palace, or when things are being taken out of it, or when drinking festivals are going on, or when the female attendants are in a hurry, or when the residence of some of the royal ladies is being changed, or when the King's wives go to gardens, or to fairs, or when they enter the palace on their return from them, or, lastly, when the King is absent on a long pilgrimage. The women of the royal harem know each other's secrets, and having but one object to attain, they give assistance to each other. A young man, who enjoys all of them, and who is common to them all, can continue enjoying his union with them so long as it is kept quiet, and is not known abroad.

Thus act the wives of others.

For these reasons a man should guard his own wife.

The followers of Babhravya say that a man should cause his wife to associate with a young woman who would tell him the secrets of other people, and thus find out from her about his wife's chastity. But Vatsyayana says, that as wicked persons are always successful with women, a man should not cause his innocent wife to be corrupted by bringing her into the company of a deceitful woman.

The following are the causes of the destruction of a woman's chastity.

Always going into society, and sitting in company
Absence of restraint
The loose habits of her husband
Want of caution in her relations with other men
Continued and long absence of her husband
Living in a foreign country
Destruction of her love and feelings by her husband
The company of loose women
The jealousy of her husband

There are also the following verses on the subject.

A clever man, learning from the Shastras the ways of winning over the wives of other people, is never deceived in the case of his own wives. No-one, however, should make use of these ways for seducing the wives of others, because they do not always succeed, and, moreover, often cause disasters, and the destruction of Dharma and Artha. This book, which is intended for the good of the people, and to teach them the ways of guarding their own wives, should not be made use of merely for gaining over the wives of others.

Sexual Union

Man is divided into three classes: the hare man, the bull man, and the horse man, according to the size of his lingam.

Women also, according to the depth of her yoni, is either a female deer, a mare, or a female elephant.

There are thus three equal unions between persons of corresponding dimensions, and there are six unequal unions, when the dimensions do not correspond, or nine in all.

The equal unions are: hare/deer; bull/mare; horse/elephant. The unequal unions are: hare/mare; hare/elephant; bull/deer; bull/elephant; horse/deer; horse/mare.

In these unequal unions, when the male exceeds the female in point of size, his union with a woman who is immediately next to him in size is called high union, and is of two kinds; while his union with the woman most remote from him in size is called the highest union, and is of one kind only. On the other hand, when the female exceeds the male in point of size, her union with a man immediately next to her in size is called low union, and is of two kinds; while her union with a man most remote from her in size is called the lowest union, and is of one kind only.

In other words, the horse and mare, the bull and deer, form the high union, while the horse and deer form the highest union. On the female side, the elephant and bull,

A carving of the kind of orgiastic behaviour Vatsyayana attributes to the young men of Gramaneri, 'one holds her, another enjoys her, a third uses her mouth . . .'.

Hindu men of status were as fond of having themselves painted making love to their wives as eighteenth-century Europeans were of posing in front of their houses or surrounded by their possessions (Pahori, Sikh School).

the mare and hare, form low unions, while the elephant and the hare make the lowest union.

There are then, nine kinds of union according to dimensions. Amongst all these, equal unions are the best, those of a superlative degree, i.e. the highest and the lowest are the worst, and the rest are middling, and with them the high[6] are better than the low.

There are also nine kinds of union according to the force of passion or carnal desire. The three equal unions are when both partners have either small, middling or intense passion. The unequal unions are small/middling; small/intense; middling/small; middling/intense; intense/small and intense/middling.

A man is called a man of small passion whose desire at the time of sexual union is not great, whose semen is scanty, and who cannot bear the warm embraces of the female.

Those who differ from this temperament are called men of middling passion, while those of intense passion are full of desire.

In the same way, women are supposed to have the three degrees of feeling as specified above.

Lastly, according to time there are three kinds of men and women: the short-timed, the moderate-timed and the long-timed, and of these as in the previous statements, there are nine kinds of union.

But on this last head there is a difference of opinion about the female, which should be stated.

Auddalika[7] says, 'Females do not emit as males do. The males simply remove their desire, while the females, from their consciousness of desire, feel a certain kind of pleasure, which gives them satisfaction, but it is impossible for them to tell you what kind of pleasure they feel. The fact from which this becomes evident is, that males, when engaged in coition, cease of themselves after emission, and are satisfied, but it is not so with females.'

This opinion is however objected to on the grounds that if a male be long-timed, the female loves him the more, but if he be short-timed, she is dissatisfied with him. And this circumstance, some would say, would prove that the female emits also.[8]

But this opinion does not hold good, for if it takes a long time to allay a woman's desire, and during this time she is enjoying great pleasure, it is quite natural then that she should wish for its continuation. And on this subject there is a verse as follows:

'By union with men the lust, desire, or passion of women is satisfied, and the pleasure derived from the consciousness of it is called their satisfaction.'

The followers of Babhravya,[9] however, say that the semen of women continues to fall from the beginning of the sexual union to its end, and it is right that it should be so, for if they had no semen there would be no embryo.

To this there is an objection. In the beginning of coition the passion of the woman is middling, and she cannot bear the vigorous thrust of her lover, but by degrees her passion increases until she ceases to think about her body, and then finally she wishes to stop from further coition.

This objection, however, does not hold good, for even in ordinary things that revolve with great force, such as a potter's wheel, or a top, we find that the motion at first is slow, but by degrees it becomes very rapid. In the same way the passion of the woman having gradually increased she has a desire to discontinue coition, when all the semen has fallen away. And there is a verse with regard to this as follows:

'The fall of the semen of the man takes place only at the end of coition, while the semen of the woman falls continually, and after the semen of both has all fallen away then they wish for the discontinuance of coition.'

6. It has become conventional for modern sexologists to play down the importance of genital size since art, or love, can overcome even extreme mismatches. Burton added the following footnote: 'High unions are said to be better than low ones, for in the former it is possible for the male to satisfy his own passion without injuring the female, while in the latter it is difficult for the female to be satisfied by any means.'

7. This is the family name of the sage Shvetaketu, one of Vatsyayana's sources who 'abbreviated' Nandi's original 1,000 chapters on love to 500.

8. Many Victorian and earlier underground writers describe female 'emission', and there seems to have been a widespread belief that women ejaculate fluid at the moment of orgasm much as men do. The persistence of this fallacy is a puzzle, as sexually experienced men could be expected to know the difference between lubrication and ejaculation. The mystery has never been satisfactorily explained.

9. This sage from the country south of Delhi shortened Auddalika's own work to 150 chapters.

This series of sensitive instructional paintings, made on cloth (above and on pages 34 and 35), depicts some of the more comfortable, less acrobatic pleasures to be enjoyed by lovers (Rajasthan).

Lastly, Vatsyayana is of opinion that the semen of the female falls in the same way as that of the male.

Now someone may ask here: if men and women are beings of the same kind, and are engaged in bringing about the same result, why should they have different works to do.

Vatsyayana says that this is so, because the ways of working as well as the consciousness of pleasure in men and women are different. The difference in the ways of working, by which men are the actors, and woman are the persons acted upon, is owing to the nature of the male and the female, otherwise the actor would be sometimes the person acted upon, and vice versa. And from this difference in the ways of working follows the difference in the consciousness of pleasure, for a man thinks, 'this woman is united with me,' and a woman thinks, 'I am united with this man.'[10]

It may be said that if the ways of working in men and women are different, why should not there be a difference, even in the pleasure they feel, and which is the result of those ways.

But this objection is groundless, for the person acting and the person acted upon being of different kinds, there is a reason for the difference in their ways of working; but there is no reason for any difference in the pleasure they feel, because they both naturally derive pleasure from the act they perform.

On this again some may say that when different persons are engaged in doing the same work, we find that they accomplish the same end or purpose; while, on the contrary, in the case of men and women we find that each of them accomplishes his or her own separately, and this is inconsistent. But this is a mistake, for we find that sometimes two things are done at the same time, as for instance in the fighting of

10. Frank Harris knew Burton and it comes as no surprise that he both read the Kama Sutra and borrowed this insight into the psychological differences between men and women for 'My Life and Loves'.

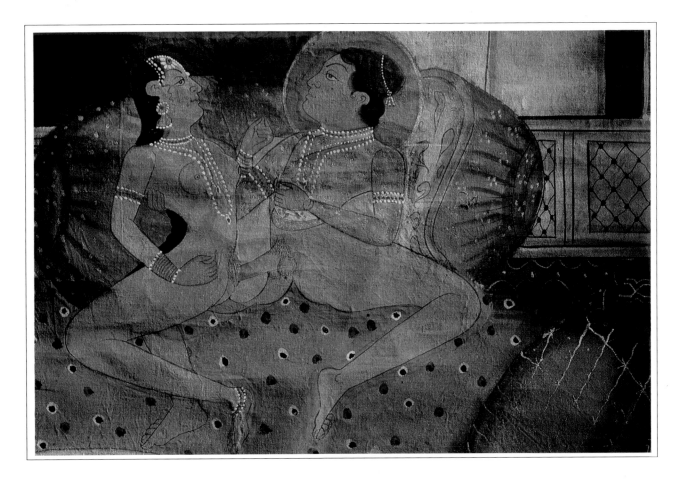

rams, both the rams receive the shock at the same time on their heads. Again, in throwing one wood apple against another, and also in a fight or struggle of wrestlers. If it be said that in these cases the things employed are of the same kind, it is answered that even in the case of men and women, the nature of the two persons is the same. And as the difference is of their conformation only, it follows that men experience the same kind of pleasure as women do.

There is also a verse on this subject as follows:
'Men and women being of the same nature, feel the same kind of pleasure, and therefore a man should marry such a woman as will love him ever afterwards'.

The pleasure of men and women being thus proved to be of the same kind, it follows that in regard to time, there are nine kinds of sexual intercourse, in the same way as there are nine kinds according to the force of passion.

There being thus nine kinds of union with regard to dimensions, force of passion, and time, respectively, by making combinations of them, innumerable kinds of union would be produced. Therefore in each particular kind of sexual union, men should use such means as they may think suitable for the occasion.

At the first time of sexual union the passion of the male is intense, and his time is short, but in subsequent unions on the same day the reverse of this is the case. With the female however it is the contrary, for at the first time her passion is weak, and then her time long, but on subsequent occasions on the same day, her passion is intense and her time short, until her passion is satisfied.

On the different Kinds of Love

Men learned in the humanities are of opinion that love is of four kinds:

1. *Love acquired by continual habit*
2. *Love resulting from the imagination*
3. *Love resulting from belief*
4. *Love resulting from the perception of external objects*

(1) Love resulting from the constant and continual performance of some act is called love acquired by constant practice and habit, as for instance the love of sexual intercourse, the love of hunting, the love of drinking, the love of gambling etc.
(2) Love which is felt for things to which we are not habituated, and which proceeds entirely from ideas, is called love resulting from imagination, as for instance, that love which some men and women and eunuchs feel for the Auparishtaka or mouth congress, and that which is felt by all for such things as embracing, kissing, etc.
(3) The love which is mutual on both sides, and proved to be true, when each looks upon the other as his or her very own, such is called love resulting from belief by the learned.
(4) The love resulting from the perception of external objects is quite evident and well-known to the world, because the pleasure which it affords is superior to the pleasure of the other kinds of love, which exist for its sake.

What has been said in this chapter upon the subject of sexual union is sufficient for the learned; but for the edification of the ignorant, the same will now be treated of at length and in detail.

The Embrace or 'Sixty-four'

This part of the Kama Shastra, which treats of sexual union, is also called 'Sixty-four,' (Chatushshashti). Some old authors say that it is called so, because it contains sixty-four chapters. Others are of opinion that the author of this part being a person named Panchala, and the person who recited the part of the Rig Veda called Dashatapa, which contains sixty-four verses, being also called Panchala, the name 'sixty-four' has been given to the part of the work in honour of the Rig Vedas. The followers of Babhravya say on the other hand that this part contains eight subjects: the embrace, kissing, scratching with the nails or fingers, biting, lying down, making various sounds, playing the part of a man, and the Auparishtaka, or mouth congress. Each of these subjects being of eight kinds, and eight multiplied by eight being sixty-four, this part is therefore named 'sixty-four'. But Vatsyayana affirms that as this part contains also the following subjects: striking, crying, the acts of a man during congress, the various kinds of congress, and other subjects, the name 'sixty-four' is given to it only accidentally. As, for instance, we say this tree is 'Saptaparna,' or seven-leaved, this offering of rice is 'Panchavarna,' or five-coloured, but the tree has not seven leaves, neither has the rice five colours.

However, the part 'sixty-four' is now treated of, and the embrace, being the first subject, will now be considered.

Servants prepare a woman for her lover: 'even young maids should study this Kama Sutra' (Rajasthan).

Now the embrace which indicates the mutual love of a man and woman who have come together is of four kinds.

Touching   *Piercing*   *Rubbing*   *Pressing*

The action in each case is denoted by the meaning of the word which stands for it.

(1) When a man under some pretext or other goes in front of or alongside a woman and touches her body with his own, it is called the 'touching embrace'.
(2) When a woman in a lonely place bends down, as if to pick up something, and pierces, as it were, a man sitting or standing, with her breasts, and the man in return takes hold of them, it is called a 'piercing embrace'.

The above two kinds of embrace take place only between persons who do not, as yet, speak freely with each other.

(3) When two lovers are walking slowly together, either in the dark, or in a place of public resort, or in a lonely place, and rub their bodies against each other, it is called a 'rubbing embrace'.
(4) When on the above occasion one of them presses the other's body forcibly against a wall or pillar, it is called a 'pressing embrace'.

These last two embraces are peculiar to those who know the intentions of each other.

Having described in some detail how to seduce the wives of others, Vatsyayana warns that it can 'often cause disasters' as in this unhappy scene (Rajasthan).

At the time of meeting the four following kinds of embrace are used:

Jataveshtitaka, or the twining of a creeper
Vrikshadhirudhaka, or climbing a tree
Tila-Tandulaka, or the mixture of sesamum seed with rice
Kshiraniraka, or milk and water embrace

(1) When a woman, clinging to a man as a creeper twines round a tree, bends his head down to hers with the desire of kissing him and slightly makes the sound of sut sut, embraces him, and looks lovingly towards him, it is called an embrace like the 'twining of a creeper'.

(2) When a woman, having placed one of her feet on the foot of her lover, and the other on one of his thighs, passes one of her arms round his back, and the other on his shoulders, makes slightly the sounds of singing and cooing, and wishes, as it were, to climb up him in order to have a kiss, it is called an embrace like the 'climbing of a tree'.

These two kinds of embrace take place when the lover is standing.

(3) When lovers lie on a bed, and embrace each other so closely that the arms and thighs of the one are encircled by the arms and thighs of the other, and are, as it were, rubbing up against them, this is called an embrace like 'the mixture of sesamum seed with rice'.

(4) When a man and a woman are very much in love with each other and, not thinking

'A man skilled in the sixty-four arts is looked upon with love by his own wife, by the wives of others, and by courtesans' (Pahori, Sikh School).

of any pain or hurt, embrace each other as if they were entering into each other's bodies either while the woman is sitting on the lap of the man, or in front of him, or on a bed, then it is called an embrace like a 'mixture of milk and water'.

These two kinds of embrace take place at the time of sexual union.

Babhravya has thus related to us the above eight kinds of embraces.

Suvarnanabha[11] moreover gives us four ways of embracing simple members of the body, which are:

11. A sage of the Mauryan period who expounded on the work of Babhravya.

The embrace of the thighs
The embrace of the jaghana, the part of the body from the navel downwards to the thighs
The embrace of the breasts
The embrace of the forehead

(1) When one of two lovers presses forcibly one or both of the thighs of the other between his or her own, it is called the 'embrace of thighs'.
(2) When the man presses the jaghana or middle part of the woman's body against his own, and mounts upon her to practise, either scratching with the nail or finger, or biting, or striking, or kissing, the hair of the woman being loose and flowing, it is called the 'embrace of the jaghana'.
(3) When a man places his breast between the breasts of a woman and presses her with it, it is called the 'embrace of the breasts'.
(4) When either of the lovers touches the mouth, the eyes and the forehead of the other with his or her own, it is called the 'embrace of the forehead'.

Some say that even shampooing[12] is a kind of embrace, because there is a touching of bodies in it. But Vatsyayana thinks that shampooing is performed at a different time, and for a different purpose, and as it is also of a different character, it cannot be said to be included in the embrace.

12. The essential business of personal hygiene was raised to the level of a ritual obligation among high-caste Hindus: the regular washing and application of scented unguents could either be performed by specialists (with the amorous possibilities which have always been associated with baths in all cultures) or among intimates of similar status as a courtesy.

There are also some verses on the subject as follows:
'The whole subject of embracing is of such a nature that men who ask questions about it, or who hear about it, or who talk about it, acquire thereby a desire for enjoyment. Even those embraces that are not mentioned in the Kama Shastra should be practised at the time of sexual enjoyment, if they are in any way conducive to the increase of love or passion. The rules of the Shastra apply so long as the passion of man is middling, but when the wheel of love is once set in motion, there is then no Shastra and no order'.

Kissing

It is said by some that there is no fixed time or order between the embrace, the kiss, and the pressing or scratching with the nails or fingers, but that all these things should be done generally before sexual union takes place, while striking and making the various sounds generally takes place at the time of the union. Vatsyayana, however, thinks that anything may take place at any time, for love does not care for time or order.

On the occasion of the first congress, kissing and the other things mentioned above should be done moderately, they should not be continued for a long time, and should be done alternately. On subsequent occasions however the reverse of all this may take place, and moderation will not be necessary, they may continue for a long time, and

A life of beauty and pleasure; with preoccupations rather different from those of the Duc de Berry depicted in Les Très Riches Heures (South India, Tamil style).

for the purpose of kindling love, they may all be done at the same time.

The following are the places for kissing: the forehead, the eyes, the cheeks, the throat, the bosom, the breasts, the lips, and the interior of the mouth. Moreover, the people of the Lat country kiss also the following places: the joints of the thighs, the arms, and the navel. But Vatsyayana thinks that though kissing is practised by these people in the above places on account of the intensity of their love, and the customs of their country, it is not fit to be practised by all.

Now in the case of a young girl there are three sorts of kisses:

The nominal kiss   *The throbbing kiss*   *The touching kiss*

(1) When a girl only touches the mouth of her lover with her own, but does not herself do anything, it is called the 'nominal kiss'.
(2) When a girl, setting aside her bashfulness a little, wishes to touch the lip that is pressed into her mouth, and with that object moves her lower lip, but not the upper one, it is called the 'throbbing kiss'.
(3) When a girl touches her lover's lip with her tongue, and having shut her eyes, places her hands on those of her lover, it is called the 'touching kiss'.

Other authors describe four other kinds of kisses:

The straight kiss   *The bent kiss*   *The turned kiss*   *The pressed kiss*

(1) When the lips of two lovers are brought into direct contact with each other, it is called a 'straight kiss'.
(2) When the heads of two lovers are bent towards each other, and when so bent, kissing takes place, it is called a 'bent kiss'.
(3) When one of them turns up the face of the other by holding the head and chin, and then kissing, it is called a 'turned kiss'.
(4) Lastly, when the lower lip is pressed with much force, it is called a 'pressed kiss'.

There is also a fifth kind of kiss called the 'greatly pressed kiss,' which is effected by taking hold of the lower lip between two fingers, and then after touching it with the tongue, pressing it with great force with the lip.

As regards kissing, a wager may be laid as to which will get hold of the lips of the other first. If the woman loses, she should pretend to cry, should keep her lover off by shaking her hands, and turn away from him and dispute with him saying 'let another wager be laid'. If she loses this a second time, she should appear doubly distressed, and when her lover is off his guard or asleep, she should get hold of his lower lip, and hold it in her teeth, so that it should not slip away, and then she should laugh, make a loud noise, deride him, dance about, and say whatever she likes in a joking way, moving her eyebrows, and rolling her eyes. Such are the wagers and quarrels as far as kissing is concerned, but the same may be applied with regard to the pressing or scratching with the nails and fingers, biting and striking. All these however are only peculiar to men and women of intense passion.

When a man kisses the upper lip of a woman, while she in return kisses his lower lip, it is called the 'kiss of the upper lip'.

When one of them takes both the lips of the other between his or her own, it is called 'a clasping kiss'. A woman, however, only takes this kind of kiss from a man with no moustache. And on the occasion of this kiss, if one of them touches the teeth, the tongue, and the palate of the other, with his or her tongue, it is called the 'fighting of the tongue'. In the same way, the pressing of the teeth of the one against the mouth of the other is to be practised.

Kissing is of four kinds: moderate, contracted, pressed, and soft, according to the different parts of the body which are kissed, for different kinds of kisses are appropriate for different parts of the body.

When a woman looks at the face of her lover while he is asleep, and kisses it to show her intention or desire, it is called a 'kiss that kindles love'.

When a woman kisses her lover while he is engaged in business, or while he is quarrelling with her, or while he is looking at something else, so that his mind may be turned away, it is called a 'kiss that turns away'.

When a lover coming home late at night kisses his beloved who is asleep on her bed in order to show her his desire, it is called a 'kiss that awakens'. On such an occasion the woman may pretend to be asleep at the time of her lover's arrival, so that she may know his intention and obtain respect from him.

When a person kisses the reflection of the person he loves in a mirror, in water, or on a wall, it is called a 'kiss showing the intention'.

When a person kisses a child sitting on his lap, or a picture, or an image, or figure, in

Polygamy made this a recurring symbol in Indian art: where a man was unable to satisfy many wives, Vatsyayana relates that the unfortunate harem women turned to 'bulbs, roots and fruits having the form of the lingam' in their frustration (Rajasthan, Jaipur).

The exuberant Grissa style of painting is a unique combination of naïveté and decadence. This luxurious couple (above and on pages 44 and 45) are practising some of love's more difficult rites.

the presence of the person beloved by him, it is called a 'transferred kiss'.

When at night at a theatre, or in an assembly of caste men, a man coming up to a woman kisses a finger of her hand if she be standing, or a toe of her foot if she be sitting, or when a woman in shampooing her lover's body, places her face on his thigh (as if she was sleepy) so as to inflame his passion, and kisses his thigh or great toe, it is called a 'demonstrative kiss'.

There is also a verse on this subject as follows:
'Whatever things may be done by one of the lovers to the other, if the woman kisses him he should kiss her in return, if she strikes him he should also strike her in return.'

Pressing, Marking, or Scratching with the Nails

When love becomes intense, pressing with the nails or scratching the body with them is practised, and it is done on the following occasions: on the first visit; at the time of setting out on a journey; on the return from a journey; at the time when an angry lover is reconciled; and lastly when the woman is intoxicated.

But pressing with the nails is not a usual thing except with those who are intensely passionate. It is employed together with biting, by those to whom the practice is

agreeable. Pressing with the nails is of the eight following kinds, according to the forms of the marks which are produced:

1. *Sounding*
2. *Half moon*
3. *A circle*
4. *A line*
5. *A tiger's nail or claw*
6. *A peacock's foot*
7. *The jump of a hare*
8. *The leaf of a blue lotus*

The places that are to be pressed with the nails are as follows: the armpit, the throat, the breasts, the lips, the jaghana, or middle parts of the body, and the thighs. But Suvarnanabha is of the opinion that when the impetuosity of passion is excessive, then the places need not be considered.

The qualities of good nails are that they should be bright, well set, clean, entire, convex, soft and glossy in appearance. Nails are of three kinds according to their size:

Small *Middling* *Large*

Small nails, which can be used in various ways, and are to be applied only with the object of giving pleasure, are possessed by the people of the southern districts.

Large nails, which give grace to the hands, and attract the hearts of women from their appearance, are possessed by the Bengalis.

Middling nails, which contain the properties of both the above kinds, belong to the people of the Maharashtra.

(1) When a person presses the chin, the breasts, the lower lip or the jaghana of another so softly that no scratch or mark is left, but only the hair on the body becomes erect from the touch of the nails, and the nails themselves make a sound, it is called a 'sounding or pressing with the nails'. This pressing is used in the case of a young girl when her lover shampoos her, scratches her head, and wants to trouble or frighten her.

(2) The curved mark with the nails, which is impressed on the neck and the breasts is called the 'half moon'.

(3) When the half moons are impressed opposite to each other, it is called a 'circle'. This mark with the nails is generally made on the navel, the small cavities about the buttocks, and on the joints of the thigh.

(4) A mark in the form of a small line, and which can be made on any part of the body, is called a 'line'.

(5) This same line, when it is curved, and made on the breast, is called a 'tiger's nail'.

(6) When a curved mark is made on the breast by means of the five nails, it is called a 'peacock's foot'. This mark is made with the object of being praised, for it requires a great deal of skill to make it properly.

(7) When five marks with the nails are made close to one another near the nipple of the breast, it is called 'the jump of a hare'.

(8) A mark made on the breast or on the hips in the form of a leaf of the blue lotus, is called the 'leaf of a blue lotus'.

When a person is going on a long journey, and makes a mark on the thighs, or on the breast, it is called a 'token of remembrance'. On such an occasion three or four lines are impressed close to one another with the nails.

Here ends the marking with the nails. Marks of other kinds than the above may also be made with the nails, for the ancient authors say, that as there are innumerable degrees of skill among men (the practice of this art being known to all), so there are innumerable ways of making these marks. And as pressing or marking with the nails is dependent on love, no one can say with certainty how many different kinds of marks with the nails do actually exist. The reason of this is, Vatsyayana says, that as variety is necessary in love, so love is to be produced by means of variety. It is on this account that courtesans, who are well acquainted with the various ways and means, become so desirable, for if variety is sought in all the arts and amusements, such as archery and others, how much more should it be sought after in the present case.

The marks of the nails should not be made on married women, but particular kinds of marks may be made on their private parts for the remembrance and increase of love.

There are also some verses on the subject, as follows:
'The love of a woman who sees the marks of nails on the private parts of her body, even though they are old and almost worn out, becomes again fresh and new. If there be no marks of nails to remind a person of the passages of love, then love is lessened in the same way as when no union takes place for a long time'.

Even when a stranger sees at a distance a young woman with the marks of nails on her breast[13] he is filled with love and respect for her.

A man, also, who carries the marks of nails and teeth on some parts of his body, influences the mind of a woman, even though it be ever so firm. In short, nothing tends to increase love so much as the effects of marking with the nails, and biting.

13. From this it would appear that in ancient times the breasts of women were not covered.

'Going out on moonlit nights', with all its voluptuous possibilities, was a social
diversion recommended to young men (Malwa, detail).

Biting (and the means to be employed with regard to women of different countries)

All the places that can be kissed, are also the places that can be bitten, except the upper lip, the interior of the mouth, and the eyes.

The qualities of good teeth are as follows: They should be equal, possessed of a pleasing brightness, capable of being coloured, of proper proportions, unbroken, and with sharp ends.

The defects of teeth on the other hand are, that they are blunt, protruding from the gums, rough, soft, large and loosely set.

The following are the different kinds of biting:

The hidden bite	*The coral and the jewel*
The swollen bite	*The line of jewels*
The point	*The broken cloud*
The line of points	*The biting of the boar*

(1) The biting which is shown only by the excessive redness of the skin that is bitten, is called the 'hidden bite'.

(2) When the skin is pressed down on both sides, it is called the 'swollen bite'.

(3) When a small portion of the skin is bitten with two teeth only, it is called the 'point'.

(4) When such small portions of the skin are bitten with all the teeth, it is called the 'line of points'.

(5) The biting which is done by bringing together the teeth and the lips, is called the 'coral and the jewel'. The lip is the coral, and the teeth the jewel.

(6) When the biting is done with all the teeth, it is called the 'line of jewels'.

(7) The biting which consists of unequal risings in a circle and which comes from the space between the teeth, is called the 'broken cloud'. This is impressed on the breasts.

(8) The biting which consists of many broad rows of marks near to one another, and with red internals, is called the 'biting of a boar'. This is impressed on the breasts and the shoulders; and these two last modes of biting are peculiar to persons of intense passion.

The lower lip is the place on which the 'hidden bite', the swollen bite, and the 'point' are made; again the 'swollen bite', and the 'coral and the jewel' bite are done on the cheek. Kissing, pressing with the nails, and biting are the ornaments of the left cheek, and when the word cheek is used, it is to be understood as the left cheek.

Both the 'line of points' and the 'line of jewels' are to be impressed on the throat, the armpit and the joints of the thighs; but the 'line of points' alone is to be impressed on the forehead and the thighs.

The marking with the nails, and the biting of the following things: an ornament of the forehead, an ear ornament, a bunch of flowers, a betel leaf, or a tamala leaf, which are worn by, or belong to the woman that is beloved, are signs of the desire of enjoyment.

Among the things mentioned above, (embracing, kissing, etc.,) those which increase passion should be done first, and those which are only for amusement or variety should be done afterwards.

There are also some verses on this subject as follows:

'When a man bites a woman forcibly, she should angrily do the same to him with double force. Thus a 'point' should be returned with a 'line of points', and a 'line of points' with a 'broken cloud', and if she be excessively chafed, she should at once begin a love quarrel with him. At such time she should take hold of her lover by the hair, and bend his head down, and kiss his lower lip, and then, being intoxicated with love, she should shut her eyes and bite him in various places. Even by day, and in a place of public resort, when her lover shows her any mark that she may have inflicted on his body, she should smile at the sight of it, and turning her face as if she were going to chide him, she should show him with an angry look the marks on her own body that have been made by him. Thus if men and women act according to each other's liking, their love for each other will not be lessened even in one hundred years.'

A detail of a painting from Malwa, where the women, according to the author of the Kama Sutra 'like embracing and kissing, but not wounding, and they are gained over by striking'.

'Congress . . . lasting only until the desire is satisfied, is called congress like that of eunuchs.'

The Different Ways of Lying Down, and Various Kinds of Congress

On the occasion of a 'high congress' the Mrigi (Deer) woman should lie down in such a way as to widen her yoni, while in a 'low congress' the Hastini (Elephant) woman should lie down so as to contract hers. But in an 'equal congress' they should lie down in the natural position. What is said above concerning the Mrigi and the Hastini applies also to the Vadawa (Mare) woman. In a 'low congress' the woman should particularly make use of medicine, to cause her desires to be satisfied quickly.

The Deer woman has the following three ways of lying down.

The widely opened position   The yawning position   The position of the wife of Indra

(1) When she lowers her head and raises her middle parts, it is called the 'widely opened position'. At such time the man should apply some unguent, so as to make the entrance easy.
(2) When she raises her thighs and keeps them wide apart and engages in congress, it is called the 'yawning position'.
(3) When she places her thighs with her legs doubled on them upon her sides, and thus engages in congress, it is called the position of Indrani, and this is learnt only by practice. The position is also useful in the case of the 'highest congress', together with the 'pressing position', the 'twining position', and the 'mare's position'.

When the legs of both the male and the female are stretched straight out over each other, it is called the 'clasping position'. It is of two kinds, the side position and the supine position, according to the way in which they lie down. In the side position the male should invariably lie on his left side, and cause the woman to lie on her right side, and this rule is to be observed in lying down with all kinds of women.

When, after congress has begun in the clasping position, the woman presses her lover with her thighs, it is called the 'pressing position'.

When the woman places one of her thighs across the thigh of her lover, it is called the 'twining position'.

When the woman forcibly holds in her yoni the lingam after it is in, it is called the 'mare's position'. This is learnt by practice only, and is chiefly found among the women of the Andra country.

The above are the different ways of lying down, mentioned by Babhravya; Suvarnanabha, however, gives the following in addition.

When the female raises both of her thighs straight up, it is called the 'rising position'.

When she raises both of her legs, and places them on her lover's shoulders, it is called the 'yawning position'.

When the legs are contracted, and thus held by the lover before his bosom, it is called the 'pressed position'.

When only one of her legs is stretched out, it is called the 'half pressed position'.

When the woman places one of her legs on her lover's shoulder and stretches the other out, and then places the latter on his shoulder, and stretches out the other, and continues to do so alternately, it is called the 'splitting of a bamboo'.

When one of her legs is placed on the head, and the other is stretched out, it is called the 'fixing of a nail'. This is learnt by practice only.

When both the legs of the woman are contracted, and placed on her stomach, it is called the 'crab's position'.

When the thighs are raised and placed one upon the other, it is called the 'packed position'.

When the shanks are placed one upon the other, it is called the 'lotus-like position'.[14]

14. Many of the love positions are derived from hatha yoga and are not easily achieved by the uninitiated. The bibliographer H.S. Ashbee reviewing the newly-printed Kama Sutra in 1885 felt that many of the love-making positions 'would seem to be impossible of accomplishment by stiff-limbed Europeans.'

When a man, during congress, turns round, and enjoys the woman without leaving her, while she embraces him round the back all the time, it is called the 'turning position', and is learnt only by practice.

Thus, says Suvarnanabha, these different ways of lying down, sitting, and standing should be practised in water, because it is easy to do therein. But Vatsyayana is of the opinion that congress in water is improper, because it is prohibited by the religious law.

When a man and a woman support themselves on each other's bodies, or on a wall, or pillar, and thus while standing engage in congress, it is called the 'supported congress'.

When a man supports himself against a wall, and the woman, sitting on his hands joined together and held underneath her, throws her arms round his neck, and putting her thighs alongside his waist, moves herself by her feet, which are touching the wall against which the man is leaning, it is called the 'suspended congress'.

When a woman stands on her hands and feet like a quadruped and her lover mounts her like a bull, it is called the 'congress of a cow'. At this time everything that is ordinarily done on the bosom should be done on the back.

An ivory carving of the 'rising position' described by Suvarnanabha.

The posture called 'splitting of a bamboo' (Central India).

In the same way can be carried on the congress of the dog, the congress of a goat, the congress of a deer, the forcible mounting of an ass, the congress of a cat, the jump of a tiger, the pressing of an elephant, the rubbing of a boar, and the mounting of a horse. And in all these cases the characteristics of these different animals should be manifested by acting like them.

When a man enjoys two women at the same time, both of whom love him equally, it is called the 'united congress'.

When a man enjoys many women altogether, it is called the 'congress of a herd of cows'.

The following kinds of congress: sporting in water, or the congress of an elephant with many female elephants which is said to take place only in the water, the congress of a collection of goats, the congress of a collection of deer, take place in imitation of these animals.

In Gramaneri many young men enjoy a woman that may be married to one of them, either one after the other, or at the same time. Thus one of them holds her, another enjoys her, a third uses her mouth, a fourth holds her middle part and in this way they go on enjoying her several parts alternately.

'A loving pair become blind with passion in the heat of congress and go on with great impetuosity paying not the least regard to excess.'

Although women's breasts were exposed at different times and in different parts of the sub-continent, they did not lose their sexual significance (Kangra, detail).

The same things can be done when several men are sitting in company with one courtesan, or when one courtesan is alone with many men. In the same way this can be done by the women of the King's harem when they accidentally get hold of a man.

The people in the Southern countries have also a congress in the anus, that is called the 'lower congress'.[15]

Thus ends the various kinds of congress. There are also two verses on the subject as follows:

'An ingenious person should multiply the kinds of congress after the fashion of the different kinds of beasts and of birds. For these different kinds of congress, performed according to the usage of each country, and the liking of each individual, generate love, friendship, and respect in the hearts of women.'

The Various Modes of Striking, and the Sounds Appropriate to Them

Sexual intercourse can be compared to a quarrel, on account of the contrarieties of love and its tendency to dispute. The place of striking with passion is the body, and on the body the special places are:

The shoulders	*The back*
The head	*The jaghana, or middle part of the body*
The space between the breasts	*The sides*

Striking is of four kinds:

Striking with the back of the hand	*Striking with the fist*
Striking with the fingers a little contracted	*Striking with the open palm of the hand*[16]

On account of its causing pain, striking gives rise to the hissing sound, which is of various kinds, and to the eight kinds of crying:

The sound Hin	*The sound Phut*
The thundering sound	*The sound Phat*
The cooing sound	*The sound Sut*
The weeping sound	*The sound Plat*

Besides these, there are also words having a meaning, such as 'mother', and those that are expressive of prohibition, sufficiency, desire of liberation, pain or praise,[17] and to which may be added sounds like those of the dove, the cuckoo, the green pigeon, the parrot, the bee, the sparrow, the flamingo, the duck, and the quail, which are all occasionally made use of.

Blows with the fist should be given on the back of the woman, while she is sitting on the lap of the man, and she should give blows in return, abusing the man as if she were angry, and making the cooing and the weeping sounds. While the woman is engaged in congress the space between the breasts should be struck with the back of the hand, slowly at first, and then proportionately to the increasing excitement, until the end.

At this time the sounds Hin and others may be made, alternatively or optionally, according to habit. When the man, making the sound Phat, strikes the woman on the head, with the fingers of his hand a little contracted, it is called Prasritaka, which means striking with the fingers of the hand a little contracted. In this case the appropriate

15. Vatsyayana, having made clear his disapproval of love-making in water because it is prohibited by religious law, resumes his usual clinical detachment when it comes to sodomy. With equal detachment, and even a little humour, Freud says of the practice: 'It is disgust which stamps that sexual aim as a perversion. I hope, however, I shall not be accused of partisanship when I assert that people who try to account for this disgust by saying that the organ in question serves the function and comes in contact with excrement . . . are not much more to the point than hysterical girls who account for their disgust of the male genital by saying that it serves to void urine'.

16. The degree of detail in this section indicates that ritualized violence was an important part of love-making in ancient India. It is curious that this most obvious divergence from Western sexual practice is largely ignored by commentators.

17. Those familiar with Lampedusa's historical novel 'The Leopard' will remember that the wife of the main character was in the habit of shouting 'Gesumaria' at the moment of orgasm.

sounds are the cooing sound, the sound Phat and the sound Phut in the interior of the mouth, and at the end of congress the sighing and weeping sounds. The sound Phat is an imitation of the sound of a bamboo being split while the sound Phut is like the sound made by something falling into water. At all times when kissing and such like things are begun, the woman should give a reply with a hissing sound. During the excitement when the woman is not accustomed to striking, she continually utters words expressive of prohibition, suffiency or desire of liberation, as well as the words 'father,' 'mother' intermingled with the sighing, weeping and thundering sounds. Towards the conclusion of the congress, the breasts, the jaghana, and the sides of the woman should be pressed with the open palms of the hand, with some force, until the end of it, and then sounds like those of the quail, or the goose should be made.

There are also two verses on the subject as follows:
'The characteristics of manhood are said to consist of roughness and impetuosity, while weakness, tenderness, sensibility, and an inclination to turn away from unpleasant things are the distinguishing marks of womanhood. The excitement of passion, and peculiarities of habit may sometime cause contrary results to appear, but these do not last long, and in the end the natural state is resumed.'

The wedge on the bosom, the scissors on the head, the piercing instrument on the cheeks, and the pinchers on the breasts and sides may also be taken into consideration with the other four modes of striking, and thus give eight ways altogether. But these four ways of striking with instruments are peculiar to the people of the southern countries, and the marks caused by them are seen on the breasts of their women. They are local peculiarities, but Vatsyayana is of opinion that the practice of them is painful, barbarous, and base, and quite unworthy of imitation.[18]

In the same way anything that is a local peculiarity should not always be adopted elsewhere, and even in the place where the practice is prevalent, excess of it should always be avoided. Instances of the dangerous use of them may be given as follows. The King of the Panchalas killed the courtesan Madhavasema by means of the wedge during congress. King Shatakarni of the Kuntalas deprived his great Queen Malayavati of her life by a pair of scissors, and Naradeva, whose hand was deformed, blinded a dancing girl by directing a piercing instrument in a wrong way.

There are also two verses on the subject as follows:
'About these things there cannot be either enumeration or any definite rule. Congress having once commenced, passion alone gives birth to all the acts of the parties.'

Such passionate actions and amorous gesticulations or movements which arise on the spur of the moment, and during sexual intercourse, cannot be defined, and are as irregular as dreams. A horse having once attained the fifth degree of motion goes on with blind speed, regardless of pits, ditches, and posts in his way; and in the same manner a loving pair become blind with passion in the heat of congress, and go on with great impetuosity paying not the least regard to excess. For this reason one who is well acquainted with the science of love, and knowing his own strength as also the tenderness, impetuosity, and strength of the young woman, should act accordingly. The various modes of enjoyment are not for all times or for all persons, but they should only be used at the proper time, and in the proper countries and places.

18. This is a terrible blunder, and one of many instances where the pandits whom Burton and Arbuthnot employed to translate from the original Sanskrit did not serve them well. Types of blow (as in the Japanese martial arts) are involved here – not metal instruments! The reference to the 'barbarous' habits of the South are typical of the early Sanskrit writers who were usually Northerners.

A mixture including ghee and honey was recommended by Vatsyayana for temporarily enlarging the yoni of a Mrigi or deer woman (Mewar).

About Women Acting the Part of a Man
and of the Work of a Man

When a woman sees that her lover is fatigued by constant congress, without having his desire satisfied, she should, with his permission, lay him down upon his back, and give him assistance by acting his part. She may also do this to satisfy the curiosity of her lover, or her own desire of novelty.

There are two ways of doing this, the first is when during congress she turns round, and gets on the top of her lover, in such a manner as to continue the congress, without obstructing the pleasure of it; and the other is when she acts the man's part from the beginning. As such a time, with flowers in her hair hanging loose, and her smiles broken by hard breathings, she should press upon her lover's bosom with her own breasts, and lowering her head frequently should do in return the same actions which he used to do before, returning his blows and chaffing him, should say, 'I was laid down by you, and fatigued with hard congress, I shall now therefore lay you down in return'. She should then again manifest her own bashfulness, her fatigue, and her desire of stopping the congress. In this way she should do the work of a man, which we shall presently relate.

Whatever is done by a man for giving pleasure to a woman is called the work of a man, and is as follows:–
While the woman is lying on his bed, and is as it were abstracted by his conversation, he should loosen the knot of her under garments, and when she begins to dispute with him, he should overwhelm her with kisses. Then when his lingam is erect he should touch her with his hands in various places, and gently manipulate various parts of the body. If the woman is bashful, and if it is the first time that they have come together, the man should place his hands between her thighs, which she would probably keep close together, and if she is a very young girl, he should first get his hands upon her breasts, which she would probably cover with her own hands, and under her armpits and on her neck. If however she is a seasoned woman, he should do whatever is fitting for the occasion. After this he should take hold of her hair, and hold her chin in his fingers for the purpose of kissing her. On this, if she is a young girl, she will become bashful and close her eyes. Anyhow he should gather from the action of the woman what things would be pleasing to her during congress.

Here Suvarnanabha says that while a man is doing to the woman what he likes best during congress, he should always make a point of pressing those parts of her body on which she turns her eyes.

The signs of the enjoyment and satisfaction of the woman are as follows: her body relaxes, she closes her eyes, she puts aside all bashfulness, and shows increased willingness to unite the two organs as closely together as possible. On the other hand, the signs of her want of enjoyment and of failing to be satisfied are as follows: she shakes her hands, she does not let the man get up, feels dejected, bites the man, kicks him, and continues to go on moving after the man has finished. In such cases the man should rub the yoni of the woman with his hand and fingers (as the elephant rubs anything with his trunk) before engaging in congress, until it is softened, and after that is done he should proceed to put his lingam into her.

The acts to be done by the man are:

Moving forward	*Rubbing*	*The blow of a boar*
Friction or churning	*Pressing*	*The blow of a bull*
Piercing	*Giving a blow*	*The sporting of a sparrow*

'Whatever things may be done by one of the lovers to the other, the same should be returned . . .
if the woman kisses him he should kiss her in return . . .' (Mewar).

There are many examples of Indian miniatures showing a great man combining hunting with unhurried sex, even while riding on the back of elephants! Presumably the intention is to record two favourite pastimes in one painting rather than anything more perilous (Rajasthan).

(1) When the organs are brought together properly and directly it is called 'moving the organ forward'.

(2) When the lingam is held with the hand, and turned all round in the yoni, it is called 'churning'.

(3) When the yoni is lowered and the upper part of it is struck with the lingam, it is called 'piercing'.

(4) When the same thing is done on the lower part of the yoni it is called 'rubbing'.

(5) When the yoni is pressed by the lingam for a long time, it is called 'pressing'.

(6) When the lingam is removed to some distance from the yoni and then forcibly strikes it, it is called 'giving a blow'.

(7) When only one part of the yoni is rubbed with the lingam it is called the 'blow of a boar'.

(8) When both sides of the yoni are rubbed in this way, it is called the 'blow of a bull'.

(9) When the lingam is in the yoni, and is moved up and down frequently, and without being taken out, it is called the 'sporting of a sparrow'. This takes place at the end of congress.

When the woman acts the part of a man, she has the following things to do in addition to the nine given above:

The pair or tongs   *The top*   *The swing*

(1) When the woman holds the lingam in her yoni, draws it in, presses it, and keeps it thus in her for a long time, it is called the 'pair of tongs'.

(2) When, while engaged in congress, she turns round like a wheel, it is called the 'top'. This is learnt by practice only.

(3) When, on such an occasion, the man lifts up the middle part of his body and the woman turns round her middle part it is called the 'swing'.

When the woman is tired, she should place her forehead on that of her lover, and should thus take rest without disturbing the union of the organs, and when the woman has rested herself the man should turn round and begin the congress again.

There are also some verses on the subject as follows:
'Though a woman is reserved, and keeps her feelings concealed, yet when she gets on the top of a man, she then shows all her love and desire. A man should gather from the actions of the woman of what disposition she is, and in what way she likes to be enjoyed. A woman during her monthly courses, a woman who has been lately confined, and a fat woman should not be made to act the part of a man.'

The Auparishtaka or Mouth Congress

19. Later in the section it is made clear that some women also practised fellatio, although heterosexual oral sex became more common in later periods: in Vatsyayana's time it was normally performed by homosexuals, either friends or servants, some of whom were transvestites.

There are two kinds of eunuchs,[19] those that are disguised as males, and those that are disguised as females. Eunuchs disguised as females imitate their dress, speech, gesture, tenderness, timidity, simplicity, softness and bashfulness. The acts that are done on the jaghana or middle parts of women, are done in the mouths of these eunuchs, and this is called Auparishtaka. These eunuchs derive their imaginative pleasure, and their livelihood from this kind of congress, and they lead the life of courtesans. So much concerning eunuchs disguised as females.

Eunuchs disguised as males keep their desires secret, and when they wish to anything they lead the life of shampooers. Under the pretence of shampooing, a eunuch of this kind embraces and draws towards himself the thighs of the man whom he is shampooing, and after this he touches the joints of his thighs and his jaghama or central portion of his body. Then, if he finds the lingam of the man erect, he presses it with his hands, and chaffs him for getting into that state. If after this, and after knowing his intention, the man does not tell the eunuch to proceed, then the latter does it of his own accord and begins the congress. If however he is ordered by the man to do it, then he disputes with him, and only consents at last with difficulty.

The following eight things are then done by the eunuch one after the other:

The nominal congress	*Kissing*
Biting the sides	*Rubbing*
Pressing outside	*Sucking a mango fruit*
Pressing inside	*Swallowing up*

At the end of each of these, the eunuch expresses his wish to stop, but when one of them is finished, the man desires him to do another, and after that is done, then the one that follows it and so on.

(1) When, holding the man's lingam with his hand, and placing it between his lips, the eunuch moves about his mouth, it is called the 'nominal congress'.

(2) When, covering the end of the lingam with his fingers collected together like the bud of a plant or flower, the eunuch presses the sides of it with his lips, using his teeth also, it is called 'biting the sides'.

(3) When, being desired to proceed, the eunuch presses the end of the lingam with his lips closed together, and kisses it as if he were drawing it out, it is called the 'outside pressing'.

(4) When, being asked to go on, he puts the lingam further into his mouth, and presses it with his lips and then takes it out, it is called the 'inside pressing'.

(5) When, holding the lingam in his hand, the eunuch kisses it as if he were kissing the lower lip, it is called 'kissing'.

(6) When, after kissing it, he touches it with his tongue everywhere and passes the tongue over the end of it, it is called 'rubbing'.

(7) When, in the same way, he puts the half of it into his mouth and forcibly kisses and sucks it, this is called 'sucking a mango fruit'.

(8) And lastly, when, with the consent of the man, the eunuch puts the whole lingam into his mouth, and presses it to the very end, as if he were going to swallow it up, it is called 'swallowing it up'.

Striking, scratching, and other things may also be done during this kind of congress.

The Auparishtaka is practised also by unchaste and wanton women, female attendants and serving maids, i.e. those who are not married to anybody, but who live by shampooing.

The Acharyas (ancient and venerable authors) are of opinion that this Auparishtaka is the work of a dog and not of a man, because it is a low practice, and opposed to the orders of the Holy Writ, and because the man himself suffers by bringing his lingam into contact with the mouths of eunuchs and women. But Vatsyayana says that the orders of the Holy Writ do not affect those who resort to courtesans, and the law prohibits the practice of the Auparishtaka with married women only. As regards the injury to the male, that can be easily remedied.

The people of Eastern India do not resort to women who practise the Auparishtaka.

The people of Ahichhatra resort to such women, but do nothing with them so far as the mouth is concerned.

The people of Saketa do with these women every kind of mouth congress, while the

*'When a courtesan consorts with men she should cause each of
them to give her money as well as pleasure. . . .'*

people of Nagara do not practise this, but do every other thing.

The people of the Shurasena country, on the southern bank of the Jumna, do everything without any hesitation, for they say that women being naturally unclean, no-one can be certain about their character, their purity, their conduct, their practices, their confidences, or their speech. They are not however on this account to be abandoned, because religious law, on the authority of which they are reckoned pure, lays down that the udder of a cow is clean at the time of milking, though the mouth of a cow, and also the mouth of her calf, are considered unclean by the Hindus. Again, a dog is clean when he seizes a deer in hunting, though food touched by a dog is otherwise considered very unclean. A bird is clean when it causes a fruit to fall from a tree by pecking at it, though things eaten by crows and other birds are considered unclean. And the mouth of a woman is clean for kissing and such like things at the time of sexual intercourse. Vatsyayana moreover thinks that in all these things connected with love, everybody should act according to the custom of his country, and his own inclination.[20]

There are also the following verses on the subject:
'The male servants of some men carry on the mouth congress with their masters. It is also practised by some citizens, who know each other well, among themselves. Some

20. Burton, in an interesting footnote explaining that the Shurasena (a 2,000-year old medical work) deals with the wounding of the lingam with teeth, makes a connection with sodomy which, he suggests, had replaced fellatio in Hindustan since the Muslim period. In 'Three Essays on Sexuality' Freud wrote: 'we must regard each individual as possessing an oral eroticism, an anal eroticism, a urethral eroticism. . . . The differences separating the normal from the abnormal can lie only in the relative strength of the individual components of the sexual instinct. . . .'

'A man marrying many wives should act fairly towards them all . . . and should not reveal to one wife the love, passion, bodily blemishes and confidential reproaches of the other.'

women of the harem, when they are amorous, do the acts of the mouth on the yonis of one another, and some men do the same thing with women. The way of doing this (kissing the yoni) should be known from kissing the mouth. When a man and woman lie down in an inverted order, with the head of the one towards the feet of the other and carry on this congress, it is called the 'congress of a crow'.

For the sake of such things, courtesans abandon men possessed of good qualities, liberal and clever, and become attached to low persons, such as slaves and elephant drivers. The Auparishtaka, or mouth congress, should never be done by a learned Brahman, by a minister that carries on the business of a state, or by a man of good reputation, because though the practice is allowed by the Shastras, there is no reason why it should be carried on, and need only be practised in particular cases. As for instance the taste, and the strength, and the digestive qualities of the flesh of dogs are mentioned in works on medicine, but it does not therefore follow that it should be eaten by the wise. In the same way there are some men, some places and some times, with respect to which these practices can be made use of. A man should therefore pay regard to the place, to the time, and to the practice which is to be carried out, as also as to whether it is agreeable to his nature and to himself, and then he may or may not practise these things according to circumstances. But after all, these things being done secretly, and the mind of the man being fickle, how can it be known what any person will do at any particular time and for any particular purpose.

'Kissing is of four kinds . . . moderate, contracted, pressed, and soft, according to the different parts of the body which are kissed. . . .'

Cushions — an essential accessory when making love on the floor — must also have prevented many millions of strains and dislocations over the centuries.

The Way how to Begin and how to End the Congress.
Different Kinds of Congress and Love Quarrels

In the pleasure-room, decorated with flowers, and fragrant with perfumes, attended by his friends and servants, the citizen should receive the woman, who will come bathed and dressed, and will invite her to take refreshment and to drink freely. He should then seat her on his left side, and holding her hair, and touching also the end and knot of her garment, he should gently embrace her with his right arm. They should then carry on an amusing conversation on various subjects, and may also talk suggestively of things which would be considered as coarse, or not to be mentioned generally in society. They may then sing, either with or without gesticulations, and play on musical instruments, talk about the arts, and persuade each other to drink. At last when the woman is overcome with love and desire, the citizen should dismiss the people that may be with him, giving them flowers, ointments, and betel leaves, and then when the two are left alone, they should proceed as has been already described in the previous chapters.

Such is the beginning of sexual union. At the end of the congress, the lovers, with modesty, and not looking at each other, should go separately to the washing-room. After this, sitting in their own places, they should eat some betel leaves, and the citizen should apply with his own hand to the body of the woman some pure sandalwood ointment, or ointment of some other kind. He should then embrace her with his left arm, and with agreeable words should cause her to drink from a cup held in his own hand, or he may give her water to drink. They can then eat sweetmeats or anything else, according to their liking, and may drink fresh juice, soup, gruel, extracts of meat, sherbet, the juice of mango fruits, the extract of the juice of the citron tree mixed with sugar, or anything that may be liked in different countries, and known to be sweet, soft, and pure. The lovers may also sit on the terrace of the palace or house, and enjoy the moonlight, and carry on an agreeable conversation. At this time too, while the woman lies in his lap, with her face towards the moon, the citizen should show her the different planets, the morning star, the polar star, and the seven Rishis, or Great Bear.

This is the end of sexual union.

Congress is of the following kinds:

Loving congress   *Congress like that of eunuchs*
Congress of subsequent love   *Deceitful congress*
Congress of artificial love   *Congress of spontaneous love*
Congress of transferred love

(1) When a man and a woman, who have been in love with each other for some time, come together with great difficulty, or when one of the two returns from a journey, or is reconciled after having been separated on account of a quarrel, then congress is called the 'loving congress'. It is carried on according to the liking of the lovers, and as long as they choose.
(2) When two persons come together, while their love for each other is still in its infancy, their congress is called the 'congress of subsequent love'.
(3) When a man carries on the congress by exciting himself by means of the sixty-four ways, such as kissing, etc., etc., or when a man and a woman come together, though in reality they are both attached to different persons, their congress is then called 'congress of artificial love'. At this time all the ways and means mentioned in the Kama Shastra should be used.

'When a man enjoys many women all together, it is called the congress of a herd of cows' (Nepal).

(4) When a man, from the beginning to the end of the congress, though having connection with the woman, thinks all the time that he is enjoying another one whom he loves, it is called the 'congress of transferred love'.

(5) Congress between a man and a female water carrier, or a female servant of a caste lower than his own, lasting only until the desire is satisfied, is called 'congress like that of eunuchs'. Here external touches, kisses, and manipulations are not to be employed.

(6) The congress between a courtesan and a rustic, and that between citizens and the women of villages, and bordering countries, is called 'deceitful congress'.

(7) The congress that takes place between two persons who are attached to one another, and which is done according to their own liking is called 'spontaneous congress'.

Thus ends the kinds of congress.

We shall now speak of love quarrels.

A woman who is very much in love with a man cannot bear to hear the name of her rival mentioned, or to have any conversation regarding her, or to be addressed by her name through mistake. If such takes place, a great quarrel arises, and the woman cries, becomes angry, tosses her hair about, strikes her lover, falls from her bed or seat, and, casting aside her garlands and ornaments, throws herself down on the ground.

At this time, the lover should attempt to reconcile her with conciliatory words, and should take her up carefully and place her on her bed. But she, not replying to his questions, and with increased anger, should bend down his head by pulling his hair, and having kicked him once, twice or thrice on his arms, head, bosom or back, should then proceed to the door of the room. Dattaka says that she should then sit angrily near the door and shed tears, but should not go out, because she would be found fault with for going away. After a time, when she thinks that the conciliatory words and actions of her lover have reached their utmost, she should then embrace him, talking to him with harsh and reproachful words, but at the same time showing a loving desire for congress.

When a woman is in her own house, and has quarrelled with her lover, she should go to him and show how angry she is, and leave him. Afterwards the citizen having sent the Vita the Vidushaka or the Pithamurda[21] to pacify her, she should accompany them back to the house, and spend the night with her lover.

Thus ends the love quarrels.

In conclusion

A man, employing the sixty-four means mentioned by Babhravya, obtains his object, and enjoys the woman of the first quality. Though he may speak well on other subjects, if he does not know the sixty-four divisions, no great respect is paid to him in the assembly of the learned. A man, devoid of other knowledge, but well acquainted with the sixty-four divisions, becomes a leader in any society of men and women. What man will not respect the sixty-four arts, considering they are respected by the learned, by the cunning, and by the courtesans. As the sixty-four arts are respected, are charming, and add to the talent of women, they are called by the Acharyas dear to women. A man skilled in the sixty-four arts is looked upon with love by his own wife, by the wives of others, and by courtesans.

21. These are stock characters in Sanskrit drama, modelled on easily recognizable types in real society. The Vita is well-educated but shallow; the Vidushaka is likeable but a clown; the Pitharmurda, a man of learning but without wealth. All fulfilled the role of go-between for the contemporary man-about-town.

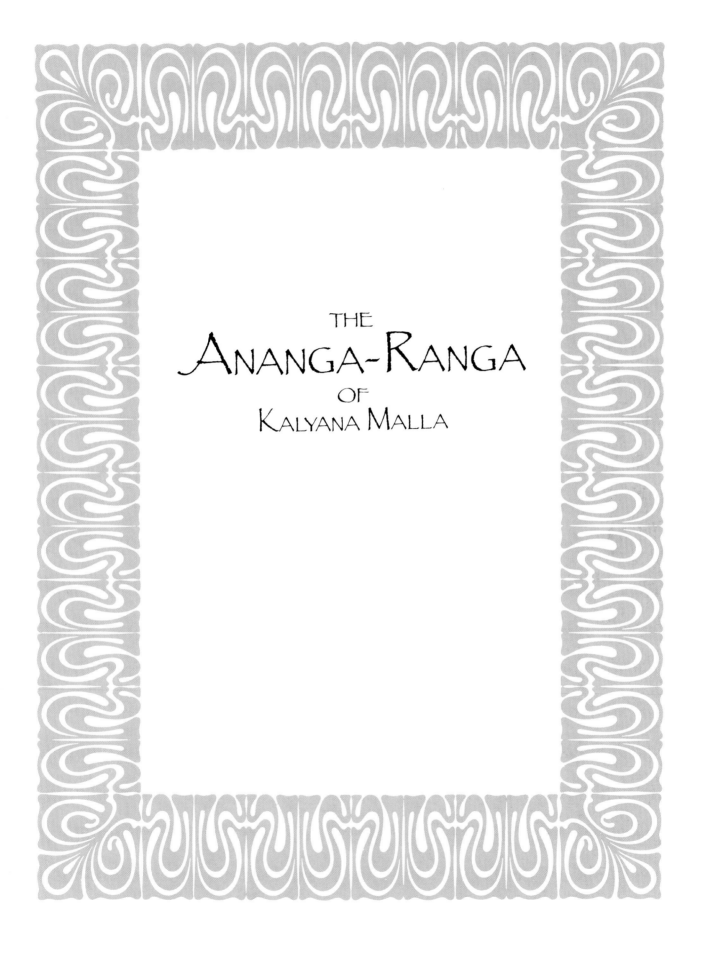

THE
ANANGA-RANGA
OF
KALYANA MALLA

May you be purified by Parvati[1] who coloured the nails of her hands, which were white like the waters of Ganges, with lac after seeing the fire on the forehead of Shambhu[2] who painted her eyes with collyrium after seeing the dark hues of Shambhu's neck and whose body-hair stood erect (with desire) after seeing in a mirror the ashes on Shambhu's body.

I invoke thee, Q Kamadeva![3] thee the sportive; thee the wanton one, who dwellest in the hearts of all created beings;

Thou instillest courage in time of war; thou destroyedst Sambar A'sura and the Rakshasas,[4] thou sufficest unto Rati,[5] and to the loves and pleasures of the world;

Thou art ever cheerful, removing uneasiness and over-activity, and thou givest comfort and happiness to the mind of man.

King Ahmad was the ornament of the Lodi House. He was a Sea, having for waters the tears shed by the widows of his slaughtered foes, and he rose to just renown and wide-spread fame. May his son Lada Khan, versed in the Kama Shastra, or Scripture of Love, and having his feet rubbed with the diadems of other kings, be ever victorious!

The great princely sage and arch-poet Kalyana Malla, versed in all the arts, after consulting many wise and holy men, and having examined the opinions of many poets, and extracted the essence of their wisdom, composed with a view of pleasing his sovereign, a work which was called Ananga-Ranga.[6] May it ever by appreciated by the discerning, for it hath been dedicated to those who are desirous of studying the art and mystery of man's highest enjoyment, and to those who are best acquainted with the science and practice of dalliance and love-delight.

It is true that no joy in the world of mortals can compare with that derived from the knowledge of the Creator. Second, however, and subordinate only to this, are the satisfaction and pleasure arising from the possession of a beautiful woman. Men, it is true, marry for the sake of undisturbed congress, as well as for love and comfort, and often they obtain handsome and attractive wives. But they do not give them plenary contentment, nor do they themselves thoroughly enjoy their charms. The reason of which is, that they are purely ignorant of the Scripture of Cupid, the Kama Shastra; and despising the difference between the several kinds of women, they regard them only in an animal point of view. Such men must be looked upon as foolish and unintelligent; and this book is composed with the object of preventing lives and loves being wasted in similar manner, and the benefits to be derived from its study are set forth in the following verses:—

'The man who knoweth the Art of Love, and who understandeth the thorough and varied enjoyment of woman;

'As advancing age cooleth his passions he learneth to think of his Creator, to study religious subjects, and to acquire divine knowledge:

'Hence when he is freed from further transmigration of souls; and when the tale of his days is duly told, he goeth direct with his wife to the Svarga (heaven).'

And thus all you who read this book shall know how delicious an instrument is woman, when artfully played upon; how capable she is of producing the most exquisite harmony; of executing the most complicated variations and of giving the divinest pleasures.

Finally, let it be understood that every Shloka (stanza) of this work has a double signification, after the fashion of the Vedanta, and may be interpreted in two ways, either mystical or amatory.

1. The wife of Shiva and Mother Goddess: here in her benevolent aspect 'Daughter of the Mountain.' In her fierce aspect – Durga, 'The Inaccessible' – her emblem is the vulva.

2. An aspect of Shiva meaning 'Self-Existent.' Lord of the Dance and Lord of Beasts, Shiva is Death and Time: his wild rhythms will destroy the world at the end of the cosmic cycle. His emblem is the phallus.

3. Kama, 'Desire,' is the Hindu Eros and son of Brahma, 'The Creator'.

4. Sambar A'sura was one of the Raksashas or demons whom Kama slew.

5. Rati, 'Pleasure,' the favourite wife of Kama.

6. 'Stage of the Bodiless One.'

The Four Orders of Women

First, let it be understood that women must be divided into four classes of temperament. These are:—

Padmini   *Chitrini*   *Shankhini*   *Hastini*

The same correspond with the four different phases of Moksha, or Release from further Transmigration. The first is Sayujyata or absorption into the essence of the Deity; the second is Samipyata, nearness to the Deity, the being born in the Divine Presence; the third is Sarupata, or resemblance to the Deity in limbs and material body; the fourth and last is Salokata or residence in the heaven of some especial god.

For the name of woman is Nari, which, being interpreted, means 'No A'ri', or foe; and such is Moksha, or absoption, because all love it and it loves all mankind.

Padmini, then, means Sayujyata, also called Khadgini-Moksha (Sword-release) the absorption of man into the Narayan (godhead), who lives in the Khshirabdi, or Milksea, one of the Seven Oceans, and from whose navel sprang the Padma, or Lotus-flower.

Chitrini is Samipyata-Koksha, like those who, having been incarnated as gods perform manifold and wonderful works. Shankhini is Sarupata-Moksha, even as the man who takes the form of Vishnu, bears upon his body the Shankha (conch shell), the Chakra or discus, and other emblems of that god. The Hastini is Salokata-Moksha, for she is what residence in Vishnu's heaven is to those of the fourth class who have attributes and properties, shape and form, hands and feet.

'The husband, by varying the enjoyment of his wife, may live with her as with thirty-two different women. . .' (Sirohi, Rajasthan).

Personal peculiarities of the Four Classes

And now learn ye by these words to distinguish from one another the four orders of woman-kind.

She in whom the following signs and symptoms appear, is called Padmini, or Lotus-woman. Her face is pleasing as the full moon; her body, well clothed with flesh, is soft as the Shiras[7] or mustard-flower; her skin is fine, tender and fair as the yellow lotus, never dark-coloured; though resembling, in the effervescence and purple light of her youth, the cloud about to burst. Her eyes are bright and beautiful as the orbs of the fawn, well-cut, and with reddish corners. Her bosom is hard, full and high; her neck is goodly shaped as the conch shell, so delicate that the saliva can be seen through it; her nose is straight and lovely, and three folds or wrinkles cross her middle, about the umbilical region. Her yoni resembles the opening lotus-bud, and her love-seed (kama-salila, the water of life) is perfumed like the lily which has newly burst. She walks with swan-like gait, and her voice is low and musical as the note of the Kokila bird[8] she delights in white raiment, in fine jewels, and in rich dresses. She eats little, sleeps lightly and, being as respectable and religious as she is clever and courteous, she is ever anxious to worship the gods, and to enjoy the conversation of Brahmans. Such, then, is the Padmini, or Lotus-woman.

The Chitrini, or Art-woman, is of the middle size, neither short nor tall, with bee-black hair, thin, round, shell-like neck; tender body; waist lean-girthed as the lion's; hard, full breasts; well-turned thighs and heavily made hips. The hair is thin about the yoni, the mons veneris being soft, raised and round. The kama-salila (love-seed) is hot, and has the perfume of honey, producing from its abundance a sound during the venereal rite. Her eyes roll, and her walk is coquettish, like the swing of an elephant, whilst her voice is that of the peacock.[9] She is fond of pleasure and variety; she delights in singing and in every kind of accomplishment, especially the arts manual; her carnal desires are not strong, and she loves her 'pets', parrots, Mainas and other birds. Such is the Chitrini, or Art-woman.

The Shankhini[10], or Conch-woman, is of bilious temperament, her skin being always hot and tawny, or dark yellow-brown; her body is large, her waist thick, and her breasts small; her head, hands, and feet are thin and long, and she looks out of the corners of her eyes. Her yoni is ever moist with kama-salila, which is distinctly salt, and the cleft is covered with thick hair. Her voice is hoarse and harsh, of the bass or contralto type; her gait is precipitate; she eats with moderation and she delights in clothes, flowers, and ornaments of red colour. She is subject to fits of amorous passion, which make her head hot and her brain confused, and at the moment of enjoyment, she thrusts her nails into her husband's flesh. She is of choleric constitution, hard-hearted, insolent and vicious; irascible, rude and ever addicted to finding fault. Such is the Shankhini or Conch-woman.

The Hastini is short of stature; she had a stout coarse body and her skin, if fair, is of a dead white; her hair is tawny, her lips are large; her voice is harsh, choked, and throaty and her neck is bent. Her gait is slow, and she walks in a slouching manner: often the toes of one foot are crooked. Her kama-salila has the savour of the juice which flows in spring from the elephant's temples. She is tardy in the art of love, and can be satisfied only by prolonged congress, in fact, the longer the better, but it will never suffice her. She is gluttonous, shameless, and irascible. Such is the Hastini, or elephant-women.[11]

7. A tall tree with fragrant pollen.

8. Usually known as the Indian cuckoo, though its voice is harsh and disagreeable; in poetry and romance it takes the place of the bulbul of Persia, and the nightingale of Europe. (Burton).

9. Meaning excellent as that of the peacock, which is not disliked by Hindus as by Europeans. They associate it with the breaking of the rainy monsoon, which brings joy to the earth and sun-parched men. (Burton).

10. Burton suggests that there is some correspondence between the four types of woman and the four temperaments associated with the cardinal humours of medieval European physiology: Sanguine; Choleric; Phlegmatic; Melancholic.

11. In the original work there now follows a series of rather pedantic tables in which the sexual appetite of the four types is related to the lunar fortnight and the eight watches of day and night. There are also tables elaborating the parts of different women to be stimulated at different times. Although the tables have been omitted for reasons of space, comments on points of particular interest have been preserved.

*Kalyana Malla's intention in the Ananga-Ranga is to promote marriage: 'that natural affection
by which husband and wife cleave to each other like the links of an iron chain'.*

The hours which give the highest enjoyment

Women, be it observed, differ greatly in the seasons which they prefer for enjoyment, according to their classes and temperaments. The Padmini, for instance, takes no satisfaction in night congress; indeed, she is thoroughly averse to it. Like the Surya Camala (day-lotus) which opens its eyes to the sun light, so she is satisfied even by a boy-husband in the bright hours. The Chitrini and the Shankhini are like the Chandra Kamala, or night-lotus, that expands to the rays of the moon; and the Hastini, who is the coarsest, ignores all these delicate distinctions. The Chitrini and the Shankhini derive no satisfaction from day congress.

The Different Kinds of Men and Women

Men

There are three kinds of men, namely the Shasha, or the Hare man; the Vrishabha, or Bull man, and the Ashwa, or Horse man. These may be described by explanation of their nature, and by enumeration of their accidents.

The more talented court painters of Rajasthan were fond of arranging copulating couples into imaginative shapes.

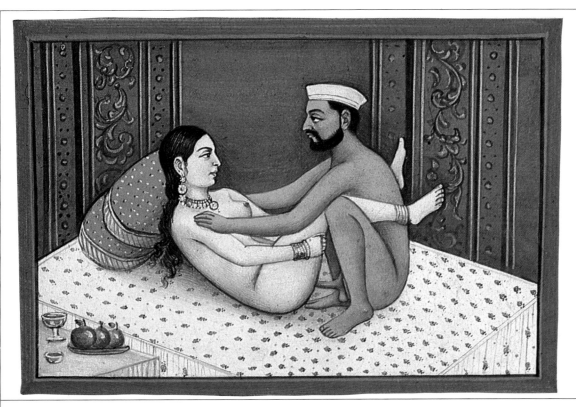

'The desires of the woman being colder and slower to rouse than those of a man,
she is not easily satisfied by a single act of congress. . . .

'Samana is when the (genital) proportions of both lovers
are alike and equal . . .' (Lucknow).

The Shasha is known by a lingam which in erection does not exceed six finger-breadths, or about three inches.[12] His figure is short and spare, but well-proportioned in shape and make; he has small hands, knees, feet, loins and thighs, the latter being darker than the rest of the skin. His features are clear and well-proportioned; his face is round, his teeth are short and fine, his hair is silky, and his eyes are large and well-opened. He is of a quiet disposition; he does good for virtue's sake; he looks forward to making a name; he is humble in demeanour; his appetite for food is small, and he is moderate in carnal desires. Finally, there is nothing offensive in his kama-salila or semen.

The Vrishabha is known by a lingam of nine finger-breadths in length or four inches and a half. His body is robust and tough, like that of a tortoise; his chest is fleshy, his belly is hard, and the frogs of the upper arms are turned so as to be brought in front. His forehead is high, his eyes large and long, with pink corners, and the palms of his hands are red. His disposition is cruel and violent, restless and irascible, and his kama-salila is ever ready.

The Ashwa is known by a lingam of twelve fingers or about six inches long. He is tall and large-framed, but not fleshy, and his delight is in big and robust women, never in those of delicate form. His body is hard as iron, his chest is broad, full and muscular; his body below the hips is long, and the same is the case with his mouth and teeth, his neck and ears; whilst his hands and fingers are remarkably so. His knees are somewhat crooked, and this distortion may also be observed in the nails of his toes. His hair is long, coarse and thick. His look is fixed and hard, without changing form, and his voice is deep like that of a bull. He is reckless in spirit, passionate and covetous, gluttonous, volatile, lazy, and full of sleep. He walks slowly, placing one foot in front of the other. He cares little for the venereal rite, except when the spasm approaches. His kama-salila is copious, salt, and goat-like.

Women

And as men are divided into three classes by the length of the lingam so the four orders of women, Padmini, Chitrini, Shankhini, and Hastini, may be subdivided into three kinds, according to the depth and extent of the yoni. These are the Mrigi, also called Harini, the Deer-woman: the Vadama or Ashvini, Mare-woman; and the Karini, or Elephant-woman.

The Mrigi has a yoni six fingers deep. Her body is delicate, with girlish aspect, soft and tender. Her head is small and well-proportioned; her bosom stands up well;[13] her stomach is thin and drawn in; her thighs and mons veneris are fleshy, and her build below the hips is solid, whilst her arms from the shoulder downwards are large and rounded. Her hair is thick and curly; her eyes are black as the dark lotus-flower; her nostrils are fine; her cheeks and ears are large; her hands, feet, and lower lip are ruddy, and her fingers are straight. Her voice is that of the Kokila bird, and her gait the rolling of the elephant. She eats moderately, but is much addicted to the pleasure of love; she is affectionate but jealous, and she is active in mind when not subdued by her passions. Her kama-salila has the pleasant perfume of the lotus-flower.

The Vadava or Ashvini numbers nine fingers in depth. Her body is delicate; her arms are thick from the shoulders downwards; her breasts and hips are broad and fleshy, and her umbilical region is high-raised but without protuberant stomach. Her hands and feet are red like flowers, and well-proportioned. Her head slopes forwards and is covered with long and straight hair; her forehead is retreating; her neck is long and much bent; her throat, eyes, and mouth are broad, and her eyes are like the petals of the dark lotus. She has a graceful walk, and she loves sleep and good living. Though

12. The penile sizes here, and later vaginal measurements, based as they are on 'finger-breadths,' must be regarded as very approximate.

13. One of Burton's footnotes from elsewhere can be placed in this chapter on physical variations. 'The women of India proper are remarkable for round and high bosoms; and the more southerly its habitat, the firmer become the breasts of the race, although we should expect the reverse, where the climate is so distinctly hot, damp, and tropical. On the other hand, the women of Cashmere, Sind and the Punjab; of Afghanistan and Persia, though otherwise beautifully shaped, and fine in face as in figure, are all more or less subject, after the birth of the first child, to the blemish of pendulous breasts. And the geographical line of sodomy corresponds with that of the flaccid bosom.'

choleric and versatile, she is affectionate to her husband; she does not easily arrive at the venereal spasm, and her kama-salila is perfumed like the lotus.

The Karini has a yoni twelve fingers in depth. Unclean in her person, she has large breasts; her nose, ears, and throat are long and thick; her cheeks are blown or expanded; her lips are long and bent outwards; her eyes are fierce and yellow-tinged; her face is broad; her hair is thick and somewhat blackish; her feet, hands, and arms are short and fat; and her teeth are large and sharp as a dog's. She is noisy when eating; her voice is hard and harsh; she is gluttonous in the extreme, and her joints crack with every movement. Of a wicked and utterly shameless disposition, she never hesitates to commit sin. Excited and disquieted by carnal desires, she is not easily satisfied, and requires congress unusually protracted. Her kama-salila is very abundant, and it suggests the juice which flows from the elephant's temples.

The wise man will bear in mind that all these characteristics are not equally well defined, and their proportions can be known only by experience. Mostly the temperaments are mixed; often we find a combination of two and in some cases even of three. Great study, therefore, is required in judging by the absence or presence of the signs and symptoms, to choose the Chandrakala and other manipulations proper to the several differences, as without such judgment the consequences of congress are not satisfactory. Thus the student is warned that the several distinctions of Padmini,

In these two Mughal paintings a European traveller is being instructed in the Hindu arts of love: judging by the position recorded in the second, he seems to have been an outstanding student.

Chitrini, Shankhini and Hastini; of Shasha, Vrishabha and Ashva, and of Mrigi (Harini), Vadava (Ashvini), and Karini are seldom found pure, and that it is his duty to learn the proportions in which they combine.

Before proceeding to the various acts of congress, the symptoms of the orgasm in women must be laid down. As soon as she commences to enjoy pleasure, the eyes are half closed and watery; the body waxes cold; the breath after being hard and jerky, is expired in sobs or sighs, the lower limbs are limply stretched out after a period of rigidity; a rising and outflow of love and affection appear, with kisses and sportive gestures; and, finally, she seems as if about to swoon. At such time, a distaste for further embraces and blandishments becomes manifest; then the wise know that, the paroxysm having taken place, the woman has enjoyed plenary satisfaction; consequently, they refrain from further congress.

Congress

Men and women, being, according to the above measurements, of three several divisions, it results that there are nine conditions under which congress takes place. Of these, however, four, being unusual, may be neglected, and attention is required only for the five following:

A celebration of many different asanas: Kalyana Malla warns that neglecting his elaborate tables for love-making may lead to dissatisfaction, adultery and even crime.

*'The woman who possesses Chanda-vega may be known by
her ever seeking carnal enjoyments . . .' (Jodhpur).*

(1) Samana is when the proportions of both lovers are alike and equal; hence there is plenary satisfaction to both.

(2) Uchha is that excess of proportion in the man which renders congress hard and difficult and therefore does not content the woman.

(3) Nichha, meaning literally, hollow or low, and metaphorically when the man is deficient in size, gives but little contentment to either lover.

(4) Anti-uchha is an exaggeration of Uchha; and

(5) Anti-niccha is an exaggeration of Nichha.

The greatest happiness consists in the correspondence of dimensions, and discomfort increases with the ratio of difference. And of this fact the reason is palpable.

There are three species of vermicules bred by blood in the yoni, and these are either Sukshma (small) Madhyama (middling), or Adhikabala (large). In their several proportions they produce a prurience and titillation, wherefrom springs that carnal desire which is caused to cease only by congress. And thus it is that a lingam of small dimensions fails to satisfy. On the other hand, excess of length offends the delicacy of the parts, and produces pain rather than pleasure. But the proportion of enjoyment arises from the exact adaptation of the lingam, especially when the diameter agrees with the extension.

 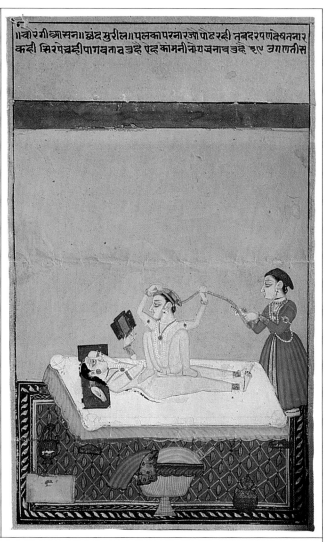

In these paintings, (above and opposite) from Central India a wealthy man enjoys the attentions of his wives and servants.

गाडरसव्यासन॥बदछरीयल॥पीउवाढौइपावपसारभरं ब्रीचानारीसुस्वाम
संभोगकरे दोजनारी जौस्वामसुजांनभरी कंवलाइकेनारीसंभोगकरी ७३॥ते
होतरमापत्र

Other minor distinctions in Congress

Each of the foregoing nine forms of congress is subdivided into nine other classes, which will now be noticed.

There are three forms of Vissrishti, or the emission of kama-salila, both in men and women, viewed with respect to length or shortness of time:–
(1) Chirasambhava-vissrishti is that which occupies a great length of time.
(2) Madhyasambhava-vissrishti is that which is accomplished within a moderate period.
(3) Shighrasambhava-vissrishti is that which takes a short time to finish.

Again, there are three degress of Vega, that is to say, force of carnal desire, resulting from mental or vital energy and acting upon men and women. In order to make this clear, a comparison may be instituted. Hunger for instance, is felt by all human beings, but it affects them differently. Some must satisfy it at once, without which they are ready to lose their senses; others can endure it for a moderate extent, whilst others suffer from it but little. The Vegas, or capacities of enjoyment, are:–
(1) Chanda-vega, furious appetite or impulse; the highest capacity.
(2) Madhyama-vega, or moderate desires.
(3) Manda-vega, slow or cold concupiscence; the lowest capacity.

The woman who possesses Chanda-vega, may be known by her ever seeking carnal enjoyment; she must enjoy it frequently and she will not be satisfied with a single

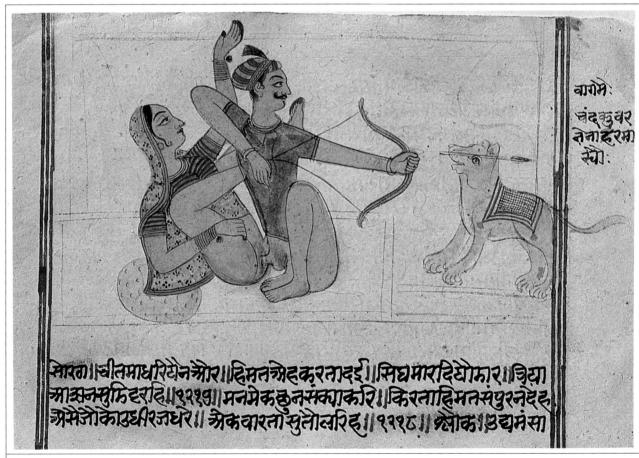

'There is no doubt about it' states the worthy author, 'monotony begets satiety and satiety distaste for congress.' He makes no mention of archery as a useful distraction (Malwar).

orgasm. If deprived of it she will, appear like one out of her senses. The reverse is she who has Manda-vega, and who seems to find in it so little enjoyment that she always denies herself to her husband. And the owner of Madhyama-vega is the most fortunate, as she is free from either excess.

Again, there are three Kriyas, acts or processes which bring on orgasms in men and women; these are:-

(1) Chirodaya-kriya, is applied to the efforts which continue long before they bear any result.

(2) Madhyodaya-kriya, those which act in a moderate time.

(3) Ladhudaya-kriya, the shortest.

Thus we may observe there are nine several forms of congress, according to the length and depth of the organs. There are also nine, determined by the longer or shorter period required to induce the orgasm, and there are nine which arise from the Kriyas or processes which lead to the conclusion. Altogether we have twenty-seven kinds of congress, which, by multiplying the nine species and the three periods, give a grand total of 243 ($9 \times 9 = 81 \times 3 = 243$).[14]

14. It is interesting to compare these early sections with their counterparts in the Kama Sutra. Although the impulse to make lists, to define categories and to number permutations is common to both the ancient and medieval works, it has become almost obsessive in the later book. The Ananga-Ranga sometimes has a quality similar to liturgy that having been too long repeated has lost something of the original meaning.

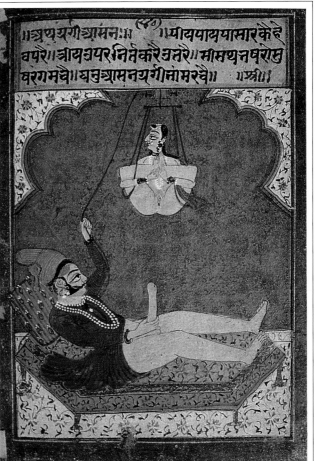

This man has a taste for dangerous methods of congress — standing postures are notoriously difficult — although he appears to have the necessary equipment to withstand disaster (Kotah).

Description of the General Qualities, Characteristics and Temperaments of Women

A woman is called Kanya from birth to the age of eight years, which is the time of Balyavastha, or childhood; and Gauri after the white goddess Parvati, from that period to her eleventh year; Tarunyavastha when she becomes marriageable; then follow Yavavastha, young womanhood, and Vreuddhavastha, old womanhood.

And further observe that there are three temperaments of women, as shown by the following characteristics:—

The signs of Kapha (lymphatic or phlegmatic diathesis) are bright eyes, teeth and nails; the body is well preserved, and the limbs do not lose their youthful form. The yoni is cool and hard, fleshy, yet delicate; and there is love and regard for the husband. Such is the lymphatic or the highest temperament.[15]

The next is the Pitta, or bilious diathesis. The woman whose bosom and nates are flaccid and pendant, not orbiculate; whose skin is white, whilst her eyes and nails are red; whose perspiration is sour, and whose yoni is hot and relaxed; who is well versed in the arts of congress, but who cannot endure it for a long time, and whose temper is alternately and suddenly angry and joyous, such a one is held to be of the Pitta or bilious temperament.

15. In old European physiology it ranked lowest. (Burton).

As so often happens, the strict and closed society of medieval India saw the corresponding development of underground licence.

She whose body is dark, hard, and coarse; whose eyes and finger nails are blackish, and whose yoni, instead of being smooth is rough as the tongue of a cow; she whose laugh is harsh; whose mind is set on gluttony; who is volatile and loquacious, whilst in congress she can hardly be satisfied, that woman is of the Vata or windy temperament, the worst of all.

Furthermore, women require to be considered in connection with the previous state of their existence; the Satva, or disposition inherited from a former life, and which influences their worldy natures.

The Davasatva-stri, who belongs to the Gods, is cheerful and lively, pure-bodied and clean, with perspiration perfumed like the lotus-flower; she is clever, wealthy and industrious, of sweet speech and benevolent, always delighting in good works; her mind is as sound as her body, nor is she ever tired of or displeased by her friends.

The Gandharvasarva-stri, who derives a name from the Gandharvas, or heavenly minstrels, is beautiful of shape, patient in mind, delighting in purity; wholly given to perfumes, fragrant substances and flowers, to singing and playing, to rich dress and fair ornaments, to sport and amorous play, especially to the Vilasa, one of the classes of feminine actions which indicate the passion of love.

The Yakshasatva-stri, who derives a name from the demi-god presiding over the gardens and treasures of Kuvera,[16] has large and fleshy breasts, with a skin fair as the

16. The god of wealth.

Tantric and other orgiastic sects flourished and artists were able to decorate their temples with erotic images of all kinds.

white champa-flower; she is fond of flesh and liquor; devoid of shame and decency; passionate and irascible, and at all hours greedy for congress.

The Munushyasatva-stri, who belongs essentially to humanity, delights in the pleasure of friendship and hospitality. She is respectable and honest; her mind is free from guile, and she is never wearied of religious actions, vows and penances.

The Pisachasatva-stri, who is concerned with that class of demons, has a short body, very dark and hot, with a forehead ever wrinkled; she is unclean in her person, greedy, fond of flesh and forbidden things, and, however much enjoyed, she is ever eager of congress, like a harlot.

The Nagasatva-stri, or snake-woman, is always in hurry and confusion, her eyes look drowsy; she yawns over and over again and she sighs with deep-drawn respiration; her mind is forgetful and she lives in doubt and suspicion.

The Kakasatva-stri, who retains the characteristics of the crow, ever rolls her eyes about as if in pain; throughout the day she wants food; she is silly, unhappy and unreasonable, spoiling everything that she touches.

The Vanarasatva-stri, or monkey-woman, rubs her eyes throughout the day, grinds and chatters with her teeth, and is very lively, active and mercurial.

The Kharasatva-stri, who preserves the characteristics of the ass, is unclean in her person, and avoids bathing, washing, and pure raiment; she cannot give a direct

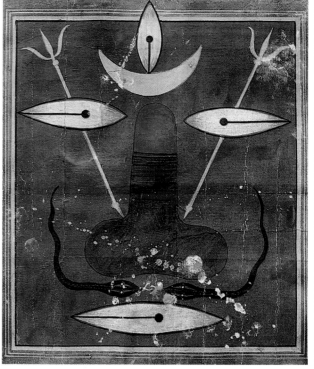

A Tantric painting whose powerful erotic symbols imaginatively anticipate Miró on the one hand and the microscopy of spermatozoa on the other.

A Hastini woman enjoys the attentions of her husband.

answer, and she speaks awkwardly and without reason, because her mind is crooked. Therefore she pleases no-one.

The subject of the Satvas is one requiring careful study, for the characteristics are every varying, and only experience can determine the class to which women belonged in the former life, and which has coloured their bodies and minds in this state of existence.

The woman whose bosom is hard and fleshy, who appears short from the fullness of her frame, and looks bright and light-coloured, such an one is known to enjoy daily congress with her husband.

The woman who, being thin, appears very tall and somewhat dark, whose limbs and body are unenergetic and languid, the effect of involuntary chastity, such an one is 'Virahini', who suffers from long separation from her husband and from the want of conjugal embraces.

A woman who eats twice as much as a man, is four times more reckless and wicked, six times more resolute and obstinate, and eight times more violent in carnal desire. She can hardly control her lust of congress, despite the shame which is natural to the sex.

The following are the signs by which the wise know that a woman is amorous:– she rubs and repeatedly smooths her hair (so that it may look well). She scratches her head

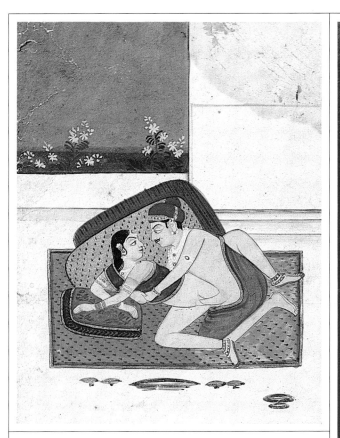

As twilight falls her husband makes haste, for the Padmini woman 'takes no satisfaction in night congress' (Jodhpur).

'What is the remedy when a woman is mightier than a man? No sooner are her legs placed wide apart, than she loses her force of passion and is satisfied' (Mughal).

(that notice may be drawn to it). She strokes her own cheeks (so as to entice her husband). She draws her dress over her bosom, apparently to readjust it, but leaves her breasts party exposed. She bites her lower lip, chewing it, as it were. At times she looks ashamed without a cause (the result of her own warm fancies), and she sits quietly in the corner (engrossed by concupiscence). She embraces her female friends, laughing loudly and speaking sweet words, with jokes and jests, to which she desires a return in kind. She kisses and hugs young children, especially boys. She smiles with one cheek, loiters in her gait, and unnecessarily stretches herself under some pretence or other. At times she looks at her shoulders and under her arms. She stammers, and does not speak clearly and distinctly. She sighs and sobs without reason, and she yawns whenever she wants tobacco, food or sleep. She even throws herself in her husband's way and will not readily get out of his path.

The following are the eight signs of indifference to be noted in womankind:– When wordly passion begins to subside, the wife does not look straight between her husband's eyes. If anything be asked of her, she shows unwillingness to reply. If the man draw near her, and look happy, she feels pained. If he departs from her she shows symptoms of satisfaction. When seated upon the bedstead, she avoids amatory blandishments and lies down quietly to sleep. When kissed or toyed with she jerks away her face or her form. She cherishes malicious feelings towards her husband's friends; and finally, she has no respect nor reverence for his family. When these signs are seen, let it be known that the wife is already weaned from conjugal desires.

The following are the principal causes which drive women to deviate from the right way, and to fall into the society of profligates:–
Remaining, when grown up, in her Maher, or mother's house, as opposed to that of her husband's parents.
Evil communication with the depraved of her own sex.
The prolonged absence of her husband.
Living in the society of vile and licentious men.
Poverty and the want of good food and dress.
Mental trouble, affliction, and unhappiness, causing her to become discontented and reckless.

The following are the fifteen principal causes which make women unhappy:–
The parsimony of parents and husbands, because the young are naturally generous.
Receiving too much respect or reverence when they are lighthearted; also being kept in awe by those with whom they would be familiar, and a too strict restraint as regards orderly and guarded deportment.
Trouble of disease and sickness.
Separation from the husband and the want of natural enjoyment.
Being made to work too hard.
Violence, inhumanity, and cruelty, such as beating.
Rough language and abuse.
Suspicion that they are inclined to evil.
Intimidation and threats of punishment for going astray.
Calumny, accusing of ill deeds and using evil words about them.
Want of cleanliness in person or dress.
Poverty.
Grief and sorrow.
Impotence of the husband.
Disregard to time and place in the act of love.

'Abhisanka is the woman whose sexual passions being in a state of overflowing . . . goes forth
wantonly at night-time to the house of some strange man . . .' (Rajasthan, Kotah).

The following are the twelve periods when women have the greatest desire for congress, and at the same time are most easily satisfied:
When tired by walking and exhausted by bodily exercise.
After a long want of intercourse with the husband, such as in the case of the Virahini.
When a month after childbirth has elapsed.
During the earlier stages of pregnancy.
When dull, idle and sleepy.
If recently cured of fever.
When showing signs of wantonness or bashfulness.
When feeling unusually merry and happy.
The Ritu-snata, immediately before and after the monthy ailment.
Maidens enjoyed for the first time.
Throughout the spring season.
During thunder, lightning and rain.
At such times women are easily subjected to men.

And furthermore, learn that there are four kinds of the Priti, or love-tie connecting men and women:–
Naisargiki-triti is that natural affection by which husband and wife cleave to each other like the links of an iron chain. It is a friendship amongst the good of both sexes.
Vishaya-triti is the fondness born in the woman, and increased by means of gifts, such as sweetmeats and delicacies, flowers, perfumery, and preparations of sandalwood, musk, saffron and so forth. It partakes, therefore, of gluttony, sensuality and luxury.
Sama-priti is also so far sensual, as it arises from the equally urgent desires of both husband and wife.
Abhyasiki-triti is the habitual love bred by mutual society: it is shown by walking in fields, gardens and similar places; by attending together at worship, penances and self-imposed religious observances; and by frequenting sportive assemblies, plays and dances, where music and similar arts are practised.

And, moreover, let it be noted, that the desires of the woman being colder and slower to rouse than those of the man, she is not easily satisfied by a single act of congress; her slower powers of excitement demand prolonged embraces and if these be denied her, she feels aggrieved. At the second act, however, her passions being thoroughly aroused, she finds the orgasm more violent, and then she is thoroughly contented. This state of things is clean reversed in the case of the man, who approaches the first act burning with love-heat, which cools during the second, and which leaves him languid and disinclined for a third. But the wise do not argue therefrom, that the desires of the woman, as long as she is young and strong, are not as full and real and urgent as those of the man. The custom of society and the shame of the sex may compel her to conceal them and even to boast that they do not exist; yet the man who has studied the Art of Love is never deceived by this cunning.

And here it is necessary to offer some description of the yoni; it being of four kinds.
That which is soft inside as the filaments of the lotus-flower; this is the best
That whose surface is studded with tender flesh-knots and similar rises
That which abounds in rolls, wrinkles and corrugations; and
That which is rough as the cow's tongue; this is the worst.
Moreover, in the yoni, there is an artery called saspanda; which corresponds with that of the lingam and which, when excited by the presence and energetic action of the latter, causes kama-salila to flow.[17] It is inside and towards the navel, and it is attached

17. The Hindus, in common with medieval European scholars, believed that men and women produced identical semen.

'Let the man, ascending the throne of love, enjoy the woman in ease and comfort.'

to certain roughnesses (thorns) which are peculiarly liable to induce the paroxysm when subjected to friction. The Madana-chatra (the clitoris), in the upper part of the yoni, is that portion which projects like the plantain-shoot sprouting from the ground; it is connected with the Mada-vahi (sperm-flowing) artery and causes the latter to overflow. Finally, there is an artery, termed Purna-chandra, which is full of the kama-salila, and to this the learned men of old attribute the monthly ailment.

Marriage and Other Matters

The characteristics of a woman whom we should take to wife, are as follows: she should come from a family of equal rank with that of her husband, a house which is known to be valiant and chaste, wise and learned, prudent and patient, correct and becomingly behaved, and famed for acting according to its religion, and for discharging its social duties. She should be free from vices, and endowed with all good qualities, possess a fair face and fine person, have brothers and kinsfolk, and be a great proficient in the Kama-shastra, or Science of Love. Such a girl is truly fitted for marriage; and let a sensible man hasten to take her, by performing the ceremonies which are commanded in the Holy Law.

And here may be learned the marks whereby beauty and good shape of body are distinguished. The maiden whose face is soft and pleasing as the moon; whose eyes are bright and liquid as the fawn's; whose nose is delicate as the sesamum flowers; whose teeth are clean as diamonds and clear as pearls; whose ears are small and rounded; whose neck is like a sea shell, with three delicate lines or tracings behind; whose lower lip is red as the ripe fruit of the bryony; whose hair is black as the Bhramara's wing; whose skin is brilliant as the flower of the dark-blue lotus, or light as the surface of polished gold; whose feet and hands are red, being marked with the circular Chakra or discus; whose stomach is small whilst the umbilical region is drawn in; whose shape below the hips is large; whose thighs, being well-proportioned and pleasing as the plantain-tree, make her walk like the elephant, neither too fast nor too slow; whose voice is sweet as the Kokila bird's – such a girl, especially if her temper be good, her nature kindly, her sleep short, and her mind and body not inclined to laziness, should at once be married by the wise man.

So much for the characteristics of the woman. On the other hand, man should be tried, even as gold is tested, in four ways: by the touchstone; by cutting; by heating: and by hammering. Thus we should take into consideration – learning; disposition; qualities; and action. The first characteristic of a man is courage, with endurance; if he attempt any deed, great or small, he should do it with the spirit of a lion. Second, is prudence; time and place must be determined, and opportunity devised, like the Bak-heron, that stands intently eyeing its prey in the pool below. The third is early rising, and causing others to do the same. The fourth is hardihood in war. The fifth is a generous distribution and division of food and property amongst family and friends. The sixth is duly attending to the wants of the wife. The seventh is circumspection in love matters. The eighth is secrecy and privacy in the venereal act. The ninth is patience and perseverance in all the business of life. The tenth is judgment in collecting and in storing up what may be necessary. The eleventh is not to allow wealth and worldly success to engender pride and vanity, magnificence and ostentation. The twelfth is never aspiring to the unattainable. The thirteenth is contentment with what the man has, if he can get no more. The fourteenth is plainness of diet. The fifteenth is to avoid over sleep. The sixteenth is to be diligent in the service of employers. The seventeenth is not to fly when attacked by robbers and villains. The eighteenth is working willingly; for instance, not taking into consideration the sun and shade if the labourer be obliged to carry a parcel. The nineteenth is the patient endurance of trouble. The twentieth is to keep the eye fixed upon a great business; and the twenty-first is to study the means properest for success. Now, any person who combines these twenty-one qualities is deservedly reputed an excellent man.

There are seven kinds of troubles which result from having intercourse with the wife of another man. Firstly, adultery shortens or lessens the period of life; secondly, the body becomes spiritless and vigourless; thirdly, the world derides and reproaches the lover; fourthly, he despises himself; fifthly, his wealth greatly decreases; sixthly, he suffers much in this world; and seventhly, he will suffer more in the world to come. Yet, despite all this ignominy, disgrace and contumely, it is necessary to have connection with the wife of another, under certain circumstances, which will be presently specified.

A woman who is 'bright and light-coloured, such a one is known to enjoy daily congress with her husband' (Deccan).

A servant waits upon a rich man and his wife enjoying their garden and each other (Rajasthan, Bundi).

Great and powerful monarchs have ruined themselves and their realms by their desire to enjoy the wives of others. For instance, in former days the family of the Ravana, King of Lanka (Ceylon), was destroyed because he forcibly abducted Sita, the wife of Rama, and this action gave rise to the Ramayana poem which is known to the whole world.[18] Vali lost his life for attempting to have connection with Tara, as is fully described in the Kishkinda-kand, a chapter of that history. Kichaka, the Kaurava, together with all his brethren, met with destruction, because he wished to have Draupada (daughter of Drupad), the common wife of the Pandu brothers, as is described in the Virat-parvi (section) of the Mahabharat. Such are the destructions which in days past have happened to those who coveted other men's wives; let none, therefore, attempt adultery even in their thoughts.

But there are ten changes in the natural state of men, which require to be taken into consideration. Firstly, when he is in a state of Dhyasa at a loss to do anything except to see a particular woman; secondly, when he finds his mind wandering, as if he were about to lose his senses; thirdly, when he is ever losing himself in thought how to woo and win the woman in question; fourthly, when he passes restless nights without the refreshment of sleep; fifthly, when his looks become haggard and his body emaciated; sixthly, when he feels himself growing shameless and departing from all sense of decency and decorum; seventhly, when his riches take to themselves wings and fly; eighthly, when the state of mental intoxication verges upon madness; ninthly, when fainting fits come on; and tenthly, when he finds himself at the door of death.

That these states are produced by sexual passion may be illustrated by an instance borrowed from the history of bygone days. Once upon a time there was a king called Pururava, who was a devout man, and who entered upon such a course of mortification and austerities that Indra, Lord of the Lower Heaven, began to fear lest he himself might be dethroned. The god, therefore, in order to interrupt these penances and other religious acts, sent down from Svarga, his own heaven, Urvashi, the most lovely of the Apsaras (nymphs). The king no sooner saw her than he fell in love with her, thinking day and night of nothing but possessing her, till at last succeeding in his subject, both spent a long time in the pleasure of carnal connection. Presently Indra, happening to remember the Apsara, dispatched his messenger, one of the Gandharvas (heavenly minstrels), to the world of mortals, and recalled her. Immediately after her departure, the mind of Pururava began to wander; he could no longer concentrate his thoughts upon worship and he felt upon the point of death.

See, then, the state to which that king was reduced by thinking so much about Urvashi! When a man has allowed himself to be carried away captive of desire, he must consult a physician, and the books of medicine which treat upon the subject. And, if he come to the conclusion that unless he enjoy his neighbour's wife he will surely die, he should, for the sake of preserving his life, possess her once and once only.[19] If, however, there be no such peremptory cause, he is by no means justified in enjoying the wife of another person, merely for the sake of pleasure and wanton gratification.

Moreover, the book of Vatsyayana, the Rishi, teaches us as follows: suppose that a woman, having reached the lusty vigour of her age, happen to become so inflamed with love for a man, and so heated by passion that she feels herself falling into the ten states before described, and likely to end in death attended with phrenzy, if her beloved refuse her sexual commerce. Under these circumstances, the man, after allowing himself to be importuned for a time, should reflect that his refusal will cost her life; he should, therefore, enjoy her on one occasion, but not always.

The following women, however, are absolutely, and under all circumstances, to be excluded from any commerce of the kind. The wife of a Brahman; of a Shrotiya

18. 'Passion Love' and its tragic consequences is a recurring theme in literature and art: Sir Herbert Read, the English critic and poet, asserted that 'only passionate love evokes poetry of the highest order'.

19. This special dispensation was known in other cultures. Seleucus, King of Syria, gave his beautiful young wife Stratonice to his son Antiochus when physicians warned him that passion was endangering his life.

The ideal wife should 'possess a fair face and a fine person . . .
and be a great proficient in the Kama Sutra . . .' (Deccan).

(Brahman learned in the Vedas); of an Agnihotri (priest who keeps up the sacred fire), and of a Puranik (reader of the Puranas). To look significantly at such a woman, or to think of her with a view of sensual desire, is highly improper: what, then, must we think of the sin of carnal copulation with her? In like manner, men prepare to go to Naraka (hell) by lying with the wife of a Kshatrya (king, or any man of the warrior caste, now extinct); of a friend or of a relation. The author of this book strongly warns and commands his readers to avoid all such deadly sins.

Indeed, there are certain other women who are never to be enjoyed, however much a man may be tempted.[20]

The following is a list of the women who can most easily be subdued. First a woman whose deportment shows signs of immodesty. Second, a widow. Third, a woman who is highly accomplished in singing, in playing musical instruments, and in similar pleasant arts. Fourth, a woman who is fond of conversation. Fifth, a woman steeped in poverty. Sixth, the wife of an imbecile or an impotent person. Seventh, the wife of a fat and tun-bellied man. Eighth, the wife of a cruel and wicked man. Ninth, the wife of one who is shorter than herself. Tenth, the wife of an old man. Eleventh, the wife of a very ugly man. Twelfth, a woman accustomed to stand in the doorway and to stare at passers by. Thirteenth, women of variable disposition. Fourteenth, the barren woman, especially if she and her husband desire the blessing of issue. Fifteenth, the woman who brags and boasts. Sixteenth, the woman who has long been separated from her husband, and deprived of her natural refreshment. Seventeenth, the woman who has never learned the real delight of carnal copulation; and eighteenth the woman whose mind remains girlish.

And now to describe the signs and symptoms by which we are to know when women are enamoured of us. Firstly, that woman loves a man when she is not ashamed of looking at him, and of boldly and without fear or deference keeping her eyes fixed upon him. Secondly, when she moves her foot to and from whilst standing up, and draws, as it were, lines upon the ground. Thirdly, when she scratches divers limbs without a sufficient reason. Fourthly, when she leers, looks obliquely, and casts sideglances. Fifthly, when she laughs causelessly at the sight of a man.

And furthermore, the woman who, instead of answering a straightforward question, replies by joking and jesting words; who slowly and deliberately follows us wherever we go; who under some pretext or other, dwells upon our faces or forms with a wistful and yearning glance; who delights in walking before us and displaying her legs or her bosom; who behaves to us with a mean and servile submission, ever praising and flattering; who contracts friendship with our friends and who is ever asking them. 'In the house of such and such a person, are there any wives? Does he love them much? And are they very beautiful?' Who, looking towards us, sings a sweet air; who passes her hands frequently over her breasts and her arms; who cracks her fingers; who yawns and sighs when not expected to do so; who will never appear before us, though we call and summon her, unless in her most becoming dress; who throws flowers and similar articles upon us; who, pretexting various things, often goes into and comes forth from the house; and finally, whose face, hands, and feet break into perspiration when she casually sees us; that woman showing any such signs and symptoms, is enamoured of us, and is strongly excited by passion; all we have to do, if versed in the art of love, is to send an able go-between.

On the other hand, the following women are hard to be subdued: first, the woman who is full of love for her husband. Second, the woman whose cold desires and contempt for congress keep her chaste. Third, the woman who is envious of another's

20. The author goes on to list twenty-four types of women who are prohibited — Vatsyayana could think of only two. With his usual pragmatism, Vatsyayana gives detailed descriptions of how to achieve adultery once it is clear that it is inevitable.

prosperity and success. Fourth, the mother of many children. Fifth, a dutiful daughter or daughter-in-law. Sixth, a courteous and respectful woman. Seventh, a woman who fears and stands in awe of her parents and those of her husband. Eighth, a wealthy woman, who ever suspects and often wrongly, that we love her money better than herself. Ninth, a woman who is shy, bashful, and retiring in the presence of strangers. Tenth, an avaricious and covetous woman. Eleventh, a woman who has no avarice or covetousness. Such women are not easily secured, nor is it worth our while to waste our hours in pursuing them.

The following are the places where a woman should not be enjoyed: first, the place where fire is lighted with the religious formula Agni-mukha and other Mantras. Second, in the presence of a Brahman or any other reverend man. Third, under the eyes of an aged person, to whom respect is due, as a Guru (spiritual guide), or a father. Fourth, when a great man is looking on. Fifth, by the side of a river or any murmuring stream. Sixth, at a Panwata, a place erected for drawing water from wells, tanks and so forth. Seventh, in a temple dedicated to the gods. Eighth, in a fort or castle. Ninth, in a guard-room, police-station, or in any government place where prisoners are confined. Tenth, on a highway. Eleventh, in a house of another person. Twelfth, in the forest. Thirteenth, in an open place, such as a meadow or an upland. Fourteenth, on ground where men are buried or burned. The consequences of carnal connection at such places are always disastrous; they breed misfortunes, and, if children be begotten, these turn out bad and malicious persons.

The following is the situation which the wise men of old[21] have described as being best fitted for sexual intercourse with women. Choose the largest, and finest, and the

21. Kalyana Malla borrowed this description from the Kama Sutra. Always an idealized scene, Vatsyayana's description was only slightly removed from reality: to the average medieval reader it was as close to his personal experience as Versailles is to ours.

A detail reminiscent of the decorative carving of the Romanesque period in Europe which offered no such opportunities for its artists.

A sadly damaged but nevertheless vivid playing-card depiction of the wheelbarrow method of coupling.

most airy room in the house, purify it thoroughly with whitewash and decorate its spacious and beautiful walls with pictures and other objects upon which the eye may dwell with delight. Scattered about this apartment place musical instruments, especially the pipe and the lute; with refreshments, as cocoa-nut, betel-leaf and milk, which is so useful for retaining and restoring vigour; bottles of rose water and various essences, fans and chauris for cooling the air, and books containing amorous songs, and gladdening the glance with illustrations of love-postures. Splendid Divalgiri or wall lights, should gleam around the hall, reflected by a hundred mirrors, whilst both man and woman should contend against any reserve, or false shame, giving themselves up in complete nakedness to unrestrained voluptuousness, upon a high and handsome bedstead, raised on tall legs, furnished with many pillows, and covered by a rich chatra, or canopy; the sheets being besprinkled with flowers and the coverlet scented by burning luscious incense, such as aloes and other fragrant woods. In such a place, let the man, ascending the throne of love, enjoy the woman in ease and comfort, gratifying his and her every wish and every whim.

External Enjoyments

By 'external enjoyments' are meant the processes which should always proceed internal enjoyment or coition. The wise have said that before congress, we must develop the desire of the weaker sex through certain preliminaries, which are many and various; such as the various embraces and kisses; the Nakhadana, or unguiculations;[22] the Dashanas, or morsications,[23] the Kesha-grahanas, or manipulating the hair, and other amorous blandishments. These affect the senses and divert the mind from coyness and coldness. After which tricks and toyings, the lover will proceed to take possession of the place.

22. Why such a ridiculous word was used for scratching is not clear.

23. Biting.

There are eight Alinganas, or modes of embracing, which will here be enumerated and carefully described.

Vrikshadhirudha is the embrace which simulates the climbing of a tree, and it is done as follows: when the husband stands up the wife should place one foot upon his foot, and raise the other leg to the height of his thigh, against which she presses it. Then encircling his waist with her arms, even as a man prepares to swarm up a palm-trunk, she holds and presses him forcibly, bends her body over his, and kisses him as if sucking the water of life.

Tila-Tandula, the embrace which represents the mixture of sesamum-seed with husked rice (Tandul). The man and woman, standing in front of each other, should fold each other to the bosom by closely encircling the waist. Then taking care to remain still, and by no means to move, they should approach the lingam to the yoni, both being veiled by the dress, and avoid interrupting the contact for some time.

Lalatika, so called because forehead (lalata) touches forehead. In this position great endearment is shown by the close pressure of arms round the waist, both still standing upright, and by the contact of brow, cheek, and eyes, of mouth, breasts and stomach.

Jaghan-alingana, meaning 'hips, loins, and thighs.' In this embrace the husband sits upon the carpet and the wife upon his thighs, embracing and kissing him with fond affection. In returning her fondling, her lungaden, or petticoats, are raised, so that her lungi, or under-garments may come in contact with his clothes, and her hair is thrown into the dishevelled state symbolizing passion; or the husband, for variety's sake, may sit upon the wife's lap.

Boredom was a problem for the fortunate few: even sexual passion can become ritualized (Udaipur).

Viddhaka, when the nipples touch the opposite body. The husband sits still, closing his eyes, and the wife, placing herself close to him, should pass her right arm over his shoulder and apply her bosom to his, pressing him forcibly, whilst he returns her embrace with equal warmth.

Urupagudha, so called from the use of the thighs. In this embrace both stand up, passing their arms round each other, and the husband[24] places his wife's legs between his own so that the inside of his thighs may come in contact with the outside of hers. As in all cases, kissing must be kept up from time to time. This is a process peculiar to those who are greatly enamoured of each other.

Dughdanir-alingana, or the 'milk and water embrace', also called 'Kshiranira', with the same signification. In this mode the husband lies upon the bed, resting on one side, right or left; the wife throws herself down near him with her face to his, and closely embraces him, the members and limbs of both touching, and entangled, as it were, with the corresponding parts of the other. And thus they should remain until desire is thoroughly aroused in both.

Vallari-vreshtita, or 'embracing as the creeper twines about the tree,' is performed as follows: whilst both are standing upright, the wife clings to her husband's waist, and passes her leg around his thigh, kissing him repeatedly and softly until he draws in his breath like one suffering from the cold. In fact, she must endeavour to imitate the vine enfolding the tree which supports it.

Here end the embracements; they should be closely studied, followed up by proper intelligence of the various modes of kisses, which must accompany and conclude the Alinganas. And understand at once that there are seven places highly proper for osculation, in fact, where all the world kisses. These are – First, the lower lip. Second, both the eyes. Third, both the cheeks. Fourth, the head. Fifth, the mouth. Sixth, both breasts and Seventh, the shoulders. It is true that the people of certain countries have other places, which they think proper to kiss; for instance, the voluptaries of Sata-desha have adopted the following formula: armpit, navel and yoni.

But this is far from being customary with the men of our country or of the world in general.

Furthermore, there are ten different kinds of kisses, each of which has its own and proper name, and these will be described in due order.

Milita-kissing, which means 'mishrita', mixing or reconciling. If the wife be angry, no matter however little, she will not kiss the face of her husband; the latter then should forcibly fix his lips upon hers and keep both mouths united till her ill-temper passes away.

Sphurita-kissing, which is connected with twitching and vellication.[25] The wife should approach her mouth to that of her husband's, who then kisses her lower lip, whilst she draws it away jerking, as it were, without any return of osculation.

Ghatika, or neck-nape kissing, a term frequently used by the poets. This is done by the wife, who, excited with passion, covers her husband's eyes with her hands, and closing her husband's eyes with her hands, and closing her own eyes, thrusts her tongue into his mouth, moving it to and fro with a motion so pleasant and slow that it at once suggests another and higher form of enjoyment.

Tiryak, or oblique kissing. In this form the husband, standing behind or at the side of his wife, places her hand beneath her chin, catches hold of it and raises it, until he has made her face look up to the sky; then he takes her lower lip beneath his teeth, gently biting and chewing it.

Uttaroshtha, or 'upper-lip kissing'. When the wife is full of desire, she should take her husband's lower lip between her teeth, chewing and biting it gently; whilst he does the same to her upper lip. In this way both excite themselves to the height of passion.

24. Note that these couples are husbands and wives. Vatsysyana's were men and women.

25. Plucking.

Pindita, or 'lump-kissing'. The wife takes hold of her husband's lips with her fingers, passes her tongue over them and bites them.

Samputa, or 'casket-kissing'. In this form the husband kisses the inside mouth of his wife, whilst she does the same to him.

Hanuvatra-kissing. In this mode the kiss should not be given at once, but begin with moving the lips towards one another in an irritating way, with freaks, pranks, and frolics. After toying together for some time, the mouths should be advanced, and the kiss exchanged.

Pratibodha, or 'awakening kiss'. When the husband, who has been absent for some time, returns home and finds his wife sleeping upon the carpet in a solitary bedroom, he fixes his lips upon hers, gradually increasing the pressure until such time as she awakes. This is by far the most agreeable form of osculation, and it leaves the most pleasant of memories.

Samaushtha-kissing. This is done by the wife taking the mouth and lips of the husband into hers, pressing them with her tongue, and dancing about him as she does so.

Kalyana Malla reminds us that a man 'approaches the first act burning with love heat: which cools during the second and which leaves him languid and disinclined for a third' (Mewar).

'As soon as she commences to enjoy pleasure the eyes are half-closed and watery . . . the breath after being hard and jerky, is expired in sobs and sighs . . .' (Sikh School).

Here end the sundry forms of kissing. And now must be described the various ways of Nakhadana, that is, of titillating and scratching with the nails. As it will not be understood what places are properest for this kind of dalliance, it should be explained as a preliminary that there are eleven parts upon which pressure may be exerted with more or less force. These are: First, the neck. Second, the hands. Third, both thighs. Fourth, both breasts. Fifth, the back. Sixth, the sides. Seventh, both axillae.[26] Eighth, the whole chest or bosom. Ninth, both hips. Tenth, the mons veneris and all the parts about the yoni; and, eleventh, both the cheeks.

Furthermore, it is necessary to learn the times and seasons when this style of manipulation is advisable. These are: First, when there is anger in the mind of the woman. Second, at the time of first enjoying her or of taking her virginity. Third, when going to separate for a short time. Fourth, when about journeying to a foreign and distant country. Fifth, when a great pecuniary loss has been sustained. Sixth, when excited with desire of congress; and, Seventh, at the season of Virati, that is to say when there is no Rati, or carnal passion. At such times the nails should always be applied to the proper places.

The nails, when in good condition and properest for use, are without spots, and lines, clean, bright, convex, hard and unbroken. Wise men have given in the Shastras these six qualities of the nails.

There are seven different ways of applying the nails.
(1) Churit-nakhadana is setting the nails in such a way upon the cheeks, lower lip and breasts, without leaving any marks, but causing horripilation, till the woman's body-hair bristles up, and a shudder passes all over the limbs.[27]
(2) Ardhachandra-nakhadana is effected by impressing with the nails upon the neck and breasts a curved mark, which resembles a half-moon (Ardha-chandra).
(3) Mandalaka is applying the nails to the face for some time, and indeed until a sign is left upon it.
(4) Tarunabhava or Rekha (a line) is the name given by men conversant with the Kama Shastra to nail-marks longer than two or three finger-breadths on the woman's head, thighs and breasts.
(5) The Mayurapada ('peacock's foot' or claw) is made by placing the thumb upon the nipple, and the four fingers upon the breast adjacent, at the same time pressing the nails till the mark resembles the trail of the peacock, which he leaves when walking upon mud.
(6) Shasha-pluta, or the 'hopping of a hare,' is the mark made upon the darker part of the breast when no other portion is affected.
(7) Anvartha-nakhadana is a name applied to the three deep marks or scratches made by the nails of the first three fingers on the back, the breasts and the parts about the yoni. This Nakhadana or ungiuculation is highly proper when going abroad to a distant country, as it serves for a keep-sake and a token of remembrance.

The voluptuary, by applying the nails as above directed with love and affection, and driven wild by the fury of passion, affords the greatest comfort to the sexual desires of the woman; in fact, there is nothing, perhaps, which is more delightful to both husband and wife than the skilful use of unguiculation.

Furthermore, it is advisable to master the proper mode of morsication or biting. It is said by persons who are absorbed in the study of sexual intercourse, that the teeth should be used to the same places where the nails are applied with the exception, however, of the eyes, the upper lip, and the tongue. Moreover, the teeth should be pressed until such time as the woman begins to exclaim, Hu! Hu! after which enough has been done.

26. Armpits.

27. The European superstition is that when horripilation takes place without apparent cause, a person is passing over the spot where the shudderer will be buried. This idea can hardly exist amongst a people who sensibly burn their dead in fixed places, so far removed from the haunts of the living; and amongst Muslims as well as Hindus, the 'goose flesh,' as we call it in our homely way, is a sign of all the passions. (Burton).

The teeth to be preferred in the husband, are those whose colour is somewhat rosy, and not of a dead white; which are bright and clean, strong, pointed and short, and which form close and regular rows.

Like the unguiculations, there are seven different Dashanas or ways of applying the teeth:—

Gudhaka-dashana, or 'secret biting', is applying the teeth only to the inner or red part of the women's lip, leaving no outside mark so as to be seen by the world.

Uchun-dashana, the wise tell us, is the word applied to biting any part of a woman's lips or cheeks.

Pravalamani-dashana, or 'coral biting', is that wonderful union of the man's tooth and the woman's lips, which converts desire into a burning flame; it cannot be described, and is to be accomplished only by long experience, not by the short practice of a few days.

Bindu-dashana ('dot' or 'drop-biting') is the mark left by the husband's two front teeth upon the woman's lower lip, or upon the place where the Tilla or brow-mark is worn.

Bindu-mala ('a rosary', or 'row of dots' or 'drops') is the same as the preceding, except that all the front teeth are applied, so as to form a regular line of marks.

Khandabhrak is the cluster or multitude of impressions made by the prints of the husband's teeth upon the brow and cheek, the neck and breast of the wife. If disposed

The pleased surprise of a housewife surprised by her husband while at her domestic duties has lost none of its humour and perception down the centuries.

The medieval love manuals absorbed many practices from Tantrism and yoga.

In some of these paintings — not necessarily the most skilfully executed — it is possible to detect the corrosive languor of a society where immolation was common. What else was there? (Jodhpur).

over the body like the Mandalaka, or Dashanagramandal, the mouth-shaped oblong traced above, it will add greatly to her beauty.

Kolacharcha is the name given by the wise to the deep and lasting marks of his teeth which the husband, in the heat of passion, and in the grief of departure when going to a foreign land, leaves upon the body of his wife. After his disappearance, she will look at them, and will frequently remember him with yearning heart.

So far for the styles of morsication. And now it is advisable to study the different fashions of Keshagrahana, or manipulating the hair, which, upon a woman's head, should be soft, close, thick, black, and wavy, nor curled, nor straight.

One of the best ways of kindling hot desire in a woman is at the time of rising, softly to hold and handle the hair, according to the manner of doing so laid down in the Kama Shastra.

The Keshagrahana are of four kinds:

Samahastakakeshagrahana, or 'holding the hair with both hands', is when the husband encloses it between his two palms behind his wife's head, at the same time kissing her lower lip.

Tarangarangakeshagrahana, or 'kissing the hair in wavy (or sinuous) fashion', is when the husband draws his wife towards him by the back hair, and kisses her at the same time.

Bhujangavallika, or the 'dragon's turn', is when the husband, excited by the approaching prospect of sexual congress amorously seizes the hind knot of his wife's hair, at the same time closely embracing her. This is done in a standing position, and the legs should be crossed with one another. It is one of the most exciting of all toyings.

Kamavatansakeshagrahana, or 'holding the crest-hair of love', is when, during the act of copulation, the husband holds with both hands his wife's hair above her ears, whilst she does the same thing to him, and both exchange frequent kisses upon the mouth.

Such, then, are the external enjoyments described in the due order according to which they ought to be practised. Those only are mentioned which are well-known to, and are highly appreciated by the world. There are many others by no means so popular, and these are omitted, less this treatise become an unwieldy size. The following may, however, be mentioned:—

The blandishments of love are a manner of battle, in which the stronger wins the day. And in order to assist us in the struggle, there are two forms of attack, known as Karatadana and Sitkreutoddesha.

Karatadana, as the word denotes, are soft tappings and pattings with the hand, by the husband or the wife, upon certain members of each other's persons.[28] And in this process there are four divisions, which the man applies to the woman:—

(1) Prasritahasta, or patting with the open palm.

(2) Uttanyahasta, the same reversed; done with the back of the hand.

(3) Mushti, or striking gently with the lower or fleshy part of the closed hand; softly hammering, as it were.

(4) Sampatahasta, or patting with the inner part of the hand, which is slightly hollowed for the purpose, like the cobra's hood.

And here may be specified the several members that should thus be operated upon. First, the flesh below the ribs, with No. 1. Second, the mons veneris and vicinity of the yoni; also with No. 1. Third, the bosom and breasts, with No. 2. Fourth, the back and hip, with No. 3. Fifth, the head with No. 4.

There are also four corresponding divisions of the practices used by the woman to the man:—

28. It is interesting to compare the relatively tame love-blows of medieval India with Vatsyayana's altogether fiercer practices.

Santanika, a name given by learned men to the act of a wife gently patting with the closed fist her husband's breast when the two have become one, so as to increase his pleasure.

Pataka is when the wife, also during congress, pats her husband gently with the open hand.

Bindumala is the name given only by men when the wife, at the time of coition, fillips her husband's body with the thumbs only.

Kundala is the name given by the older poets when the wife, during copulation, fillips her husband's body with thumb and fore-finger, not with the rest of the hand.

And now of the Sitkriti, or inarticulate sound produced by drawing in the breath between the closed teeth; these are the peculiar privilege and prerogative of women, and the wise divide them into five kinds:—

Hinkriti is the deep and grave sound, like 'Hun! hun hun!' 'Hin! hin! hin!' produced in the nose and mouth with the slightest use of the former member.

Stanita is the low rumbling, like distant thunder expressed by 'Ha! ha!' or by 'Han! han! han!' produced by the throat without the concurrence of the nasal muscles.

Sitkriti is the expiration or emission of breath, like the hissing of a serpent, expressed by 'Shan! shan!' or 'Shish! shish!' and produced only in the mouth.

Utkriti is the cracking sound, resembling the splitting of a bamboo, expressed by 'T'hat! t'hat!' and formed by applying the tongue-tip to the palate, and by moving it as rapidly as possible, at the same time pronouncing the interjection.

Bhavakriti is a rattling sound, like the fall of heavy rain-drops, expressed by 'T'hap! t'hap!' produced by the lips; but it can be produced only at the time of congress.

These several Sitkritis in the woman's mouth at the moment of enjoyment, will respectively resemble the cry of the quail (Lava), of the Indian cuckoo (Kokila), of the spotted-necked pigeon (Kapota), of the Hansa-goose and of the peacock. The sounds should especially be produced when the husband kisses, bites, and chews his wife's lower lip; and the sweetness of the utterance greatly adds to enjoyment, and promotes the congress of the sexual act.

Furthermore, be it known to men the peculiar characteristics of the Ashtamahanayika, or the eight great forms of Nayika:—[29]

(1) Khanditanayika, when the husband bears upon his body all the marks of sexual enjoyment, produced by sleeping with a rival wife; and when, with eyes reddened by keeping late hours, he returns to his beloved struck with fear and in an agitated state, coaxing her, and speaking sweet words, for the purpose of sueing her to congress, and she half listens to him, but yields at last. Such is the name given to her by the great poets of the olden time.

(2) Vasakasajjita is the word applied by the learned to the wife, who, having spread a soft, fine bed, in a charming apartment, sits upon it at night-time, and awaits her husband, with great expectation, now half closing her eyes, then fixing her glance on the door.

(3) Kalakantarita, say wise men, is the term for a wife, who when her husband, after grossly injuring her, falls at her feet and begs for pardon, answers him loudly and in great wrath, drives him from her presence, and determines not to see him again; but presently, waxing repentant, laments in various ways the pains and sorrows of separation and at last recovers quietude by the hope of reunion.

(4) Abhisarika is the woman whose sexual passions being in a state of overflowing, dresses herself, and goes forth shamelessly, and wantonly at night-time to the house of some strange man, in the hope of carnal copulation with him.

29. A mistress or lover: the eight types of woman are borrowed from the stereotypes of Hindu drama.

The contemporary equivalent of an executive toy (Jaipur).

(5) Vipralabdha is the disappointed woman, who, having sent a go-between to some strange man, appointing him to meet her at a certain place, repairs there, confused and agitated with the prospect of congress, but sees the go-between returning alone, and without the lover, which throws her into a state of fever.

(6) Viyogini is the melancholy woman, who, during the absence of her husband in a far country, smells the fragrant and exciting perfumes of sandalwood, and other odorous substances and looking upon the lotus-flower and the moonlight, falls into a passion of grief.

(7) Svadhinapurvapatika is the name given to the wife whose husband instead of gratifying her amorous desires, and studying her carnal wants, engages in the pursuit of philosophic knowledge derived from meditation.

(8) Utkanthita, according to the best poets, is the woman who loves her husband very dearly, whose eyes are light and lively, who has decorated herself with jewels and garlands, well knowing the wishes of her man, and who, burning with desire, awaits his coming, propped up with pillows in a sleeping-apartment appropriated to pleasure and sumptuously adorned with mirrors and pictures.

Internal Enjoyments in its Various Forms

By 'internal enjoyment' is meant the art of congress which follows the various external preliminaries described in the last chapter. These embraces, kisses and sundry manipulations, must always be practised according to the taste of husband and wife, and if persisted in as the Shastra directs, they will excessively excite the passions of the woman, and will soften and loosen her yoni so as to be ready for carnal connection.

The following verses show how much art and science there is in a matter which appears so simple to the uneducated and vulgar:

'What is the remedy when a woman is mightier that a man? Although she be very strong, yet no sooner are her legs placed wide apart, then she loses her force of passion, and is satisfied.'

'Thus the yoni from being tight and compact, becomes slack and loose; let the husband, therefore, press her thighs together, and she will be equally able to struggle with him at the time of congress.'

'Well, if a woman be only twelve or thirteen years old, and the man is quite grown up, and has lost the first vigour of his youth, what must be done to make them equal?'

'In such a case, the legs of the woman must be stretched out to the fullest extent, so as to weaken the powers, and by these means the man will prove himself her equal.'

There are five main Bandha or A'sana – forms or postures of congress, and each of these will require its own description successively, and in due order.

Uttana-bandha (supine posture) is the great division so-called by men well versed in the Art of Love, when a woman lies upon her back, and her husband sits close to her upon his hams. But is this all that can be said of it? No! no! there are eleven subdivisions:

(1) Samapada-uttana-bandha, is when the husband places his wife upon her back, raises both her legs, and placing them upon his shoulders, sits close to her and enjoys her.

(2) Nagara-uttana-bandha, is when the husband places his wife upon her back, sits between her legs, raises them both, keeping them on the other side of his waist, and thus enjoys her.

(3) Traivikrama-uttana-bandha, is when one of the wife's legs is left lying upon the bed or carpet, the other being placed upon the head of the husband, who supports himself upon both hands. This position is very admirable.

(4) Vyomapada-uttana-bandha, is when the wife, lying upon her back, raises with her hands both legs, drawing them as far back as her hair; the husband then sitting close to her, places both hands upon her breasts and enjoys her.

(5) Smarachakrasana, or the position of the Kama's wheel, a mode very much enjoyed by the voluptuary. In this form, the husband sits between the legs of his wife, extends his arms on both sides of her as far as he can, and thus enjoys her.

(6) Avidarita is that position when the wife raises both her legs, so that they may touch the bosom of her husband, who, sitting between her thighs, embraces and enjoys her.

(7) Saumya-bandha is the name given by the old poets to a form of congress much in vogue amongst the artful students of the Kama Shastra. The wife lies supine, and the husband, as usual, sits; he places both hands under her back, closely embracing her, which she returns by tightly grasping his neck.

(8) Jrimbhita-asana. In order to bend the wife's body in the form of a bow, the husband places little pillows or pads beneath her hips and head, he then raises the seat of pleasure and rises to it by kneeling upon a cushion. This is an admirable form of congress, and is greatly enjoyed by both.

(9) Veshtita-asana is when the wife lies upon her back cross-legged, and raises her feet a little; this position is very well fitted for those burning with desire.

'Women require to be considered in connection with the previous state of their existence: the Satva or disposition inherited from a former life.'

(10) Venuvidarita is that in which the wife, lying upon her back, places one leg upon her husband's shoulder, and the other on the bed or carpet.

(11) Sphutma-uttana-bandha is when the husband, after insertion and penetration, raises the legs of his wife, who still lies upon her back, and joins her thighs closely together.

Here end the eleven forms of Uttana-bandha; we now proceed to the Tiryak (aslant, awry posture) whose essence consists of the woman lying upon her side. Of this division, there are three sub-divisions:—

(1) Vinaka-tiryak-bandha is when the husband, placing himself alongside of his wife, raises one of his legs over her hip and leaves the other lying upon the bed or carpet. This A'sana (position) is fitted only for practice upon a grown-up woman; in the case of a younger person, the result is by no means satisfactory.

(2) Samputa-tiryak-bandha is when both man and woman lie straight upon their sides, without any movement or change in the position of their limbs.

(3) Karkata-tiryak-bandha is when both being upon their sides, the husband lies between his wife's thighs, one under him, and the other being thrown over his flank, a little below the breast.

Here end the three forms of the Tiryak-bandha; and we now proceed to the Upavishta (sitting) posture. Of this division there are ten sub-divisions.

(1) Padm-asana. The husband in this favourite position sits cross-legged upon the bed or carpet, and takes his wife upon his lap, placing his hands upon her shoulders.

Nepal was one of the main centres of Tantrism, which teaches that perfection is achieved by satisfying all desire.

It may be an unconscious effect on the part of the artist, but this pair look as if surprised in illicit union – something which attracts the author's strongest invective.

(2) Upapad-asana. In this posture, whilst both are sitting, the woman slightly raises one leg by placing the hand under it, and the husband enjoys her.

(3) Vaidhurit-asana. The husband embraces his wife's neck very closely, and she does the same to him.

(4) Phanipash-asana. The husband holds his wife's feet, and the wife those of her husband.

(5) Sanyaman-asana. The husband passes both the legs of his wife under his arms at the elbow, and holds her neck with his hands.

(6) Kaurmak-asana (of the tortoise posture). The husband must so sit that his mouth, arms, and legs touch the corresponding members of his wife.

(7) Parivartit-asana. In addition to the mutual contact of mouth, arms, and legs, the husband must frequently pass both the legs of his wife under his arms at the elbow.

(8) Yugmapad-asana is a name given by the poets to that position in which the husband sits with his legs wide apart, and, after insertion and penetration, presses the thighs of his wife together.

(9) Vinarditasana, a form possible only to a very strong man with a very light woman; he raises her by passing both her legs over his arms at the elbow, and moves her about from left to right, but not backwards or forwards, till the supreme moment arrives.

(10) Markatasana, is the same position as No. 9; in this, however, the husband moves the wife in a straight line away from his face, that is, backwards and forwards, but not from side to side.

Here end the forms of Upavishta, or sitting-posture. The next is Utthita, (the standing posture) which admits of three sub-divisions:—

(1) Janu-kuru-utthitha-bandha (that is, 'knee and elbow standing-form') a posture which also requires great bodily strength in the man. Both stand opposite to each other, and the husband passes his two arms under his wife's knees, supporting her upon the inner elbows; he then raises her as high as his waist, and enjoys her, whilst she must clasp his neck with both her hands.

(2) Hari-vikrama-utthita-bandha; in this form the husband raises only one leg of his wife, who with the other stands upon the ground. It is a position delightful to young women.

(3) Kirti-utthita-bandha: this require strength in the man, but not so much as is wanted for the first sub-division. The wife, clasping her hands and placing her legs round her husband's waist, hangs, as it were, to him, whilst he supports her by placing his fore arms under her hips.

Here end the forms of Utthita, or standing-posture; and now we come to the Vyanta-bandha, which means congress with a woman when she is prone, that is, with the breast and stomach to the bed or carpet. Of this A'sana, there are only two well-known sub-divisions:—

(1) Dhenuka-vyanta-bandha (the cow posture): in this position the wife places herself upon all fours, supported on her hands and feet (not her knees), and the husband, approaching from behind, falls upon her waist, and enjoys her as if he were a bull. There is much religious merit in this form.[30]

(2) Aybha-vyanta-bandha (or Gajasawa, the elephant posture). The wife lies down in such a position that her face, breast, stomach, and thighs all touch the bed or carpet, and the husband, extending himself upon her, and bending himself like an elephant, with the small of the back much drawn in, works underneath her, and effects insertion.

'O Rajah,' said the arch-poet Kalyana-Malla, 'there are many other forms of congress, such as Harinasana, Sukrasana, Gardhabasana, and so forth; but they are not

30. Presumably this is a joke inserted by Burton – for Hindus of course, the cow is sacred.

known to the people, and being useless as well as very difficult of performance, nay, sometimes so full of faults as to be excluded or prohibited, I have, therefore, not related them to you. But if you desire to hear anything more about postures, be pleased to ask, and your servant will attempt to satisfy your curiosity.'

'Right well!' exclaimed the king. 'I much wish to hear you describe the Purushayitabandha.'

'Hear, O Rajah,' resumed the poet, 'whilst I relate all that requires to be known concerning that form of congress.'

Purushayitabandha is the reverse of what men usually practise. In this case the man lies upon his back, draws his wife upon him and enjoys her. It is especially useful when he, being exhausted, is no longer capable of muscular exertion, and when she is ungratified, being still full of the water of love. The wife must, therefore, place her husband supine upon the bed or carpet, mount upon his person, and satisfy her desires. Of this form of congress there are three sub-divisions:–

(1) Viparita-bandha, or 'contrary position', is when the wife lies straight upon the outstretched person of her husband, her breast being applied to his bosom, presses his waist with her hands, and moving her hips sharply in various directions, enjoys him.

(2) Purushayita-bhramara-bandha ('like the large bee'): in this, the wife, having placed her husband at full length upon the bed or carpet, sits at squat upon his thighs, closes her legs firmly after she has effected insertion; and, moving her waist in a circular form, churning, as it were, enjoys her husband, and thoroughly satisfies herself.

(3) Utthita-uttana-bandha. The wife, whose passion has not been gratified by previous copulation, should make her husband lie upon his back, and sitting cross-legged upon his thighs, should seize his lingam, effect insertion, and move her waist up and down, advancing and retiring; she will derive great comfort from this process.

Whilst thus reversing the natural order in all these forms of Purushayita, the wife will draw in her breath after the fashion called Sitkara; she will smile gently, and she will show a kind of half shame, making her face so attractive that it cannot well be described. After which she will say to her husband, 'Oh my dear! Oh thou rogue; this day thou hast come under my control, and hast become subjected to me, being totally defeated in the battle of love!' Her husband manipulates her hair according to art, embraces her and kisses her lower lip; whereupon all her members will relax, she will close her eyes and fall into a swoon of joy.

Moreover, at all times of enjoying Purushayita the wife will remember that without an especial exertion of will on her part, the husband's pleasure will not be perfect. To this end she must ever strive to close and constrict the yoni until it holds the lingam, as, with a finger, opening and shutting at her pleasure, and finally, acting as the hand of the Gopala-girl, who milks the cow. This can be learned only by long practice, and especially by throwing the will into the part to be affected, even as men endeavour to sharpen their hearing, and their sense of touch. While so doing, she will mentally repeat 'Kamadeva! Kamadeva', in order that a blessing may rest upon the undertaking. And she will be pleased to hear that the act once learned, is never lost. Her husband will then value her above all women, nor would he exchange her for the most beautiful Rani (queen) in the three worlds. So lovely and pleasant to man is she who constricts.

Let it now be observed that there are sundry kinds and conditions of women whom the wise peremptorily exclude from Purushayita, and the principal exceptions will here be mentioned. First, the Karini-woman. Second, the Harini. Third, she who is pregnant. Fourth, she who has not long left the lying-in chamber. Fifth, a woman of thin and lean body, because the exertion will be too great for her strength. Sixth, a woman suffering from fever or other weakening complaint. Seventh, a virgin; and, eighth, a girl not yet arrived at puberty.

The standing postures, Utthita, require considerable strength on the man's part — literally.

And now having duly concluded the chapter of internal enjoyments, it is good to know that if husband and wife live togther in close agreement, as one soul in a single body, they shall be happy in this world, and in that to come. Their good and charitable actions will be an example to mankind, and their peace and harmony will effect their salvation. No-one yet has written a book to prevent the separation of the married pair and to show them how they may pass through life in union. Seeing this, I felt compassion, and composed the treatise, offering it to the god Pandurang.

The chief reason for the separation between the married couple and the cause, which drives the husband to the embraces of strange women, and the wife to the arms of strange men, is the want of varied pleasures and the monotony which follows possession. There is no doubt about it. Monotony begets satiety, and satiety distaste for congress, especially in one or the other; malicious feelings are engendered, the husband or the wife yields to temptation, and the other follows, being driven by jealousy. For it seldom happens that the two love each other equally, and in exact proportion, therefore is the one more easily seduced by passion than the other. From such separations result polygamy, adulteries, abortions, and every manner of vice, and not only do the erring husband and wife fall into the pit, but they also drag down the names of their deceased ancestors from the place of beautiful mortals, either to hell or back again upon this world. Fully understanding the way in which such quarrels arise, I have in this book shown how the husband, by varying the enjoyment of his wife, may live with her as with thirty-two different women, ever varying the enjoyment of her, and rendering satiety impossible. I have also taught all manner of useful arts and mysteries, by which she may render herself pure, beautiful and pleasing in his eyes. Let me, therefore, conclude with the verse of blessing:–

'May this treatise,
'Ananga-ranga', be be-
loved of Man and Woman, as
long as the Holy River Ganges
springeth from Shiva, with his
wife Gauri on his left side; as long as
Lakshmi loveth Vishnu; as long
as Bramha is engaged in the
study of the Vedas; and as
long as the Earth, the
Moon and the Sun
endure.'

THE
PERFUMED GARDEN
OF
SHEIKH NEFZAWI

Praise be to God who had placed the source of man's greatest pleasure in woman's natural parts, and woman's greatest pleasure in the natural parts of man!

Who has decreed that the well-being, satisfaction and comfort of a woman's parts shall depend on the welcome they accord to the virile member, and that a man shall know neither rest nor peace till his duty has been nobly done!

When the mutual operation is performed, a lively combat ensues between the two actors who frolic and kiss and intertwine. Enjoyment is not long delayed, in consequence of the contact of the two pubes. Man, in the pride of his strength, works like a pestle, and woman, with lascivious undulations, comes artfully to his aid. Soon, all too soon, the ejaculation comes!

God has granted us the kiss on the mouth, the cheeks and the neck, as also the sucking of luscious lips, to provoke an erection at a favourable time. It is He, who, in His wisdom, has embellished with breasts a woman's chest, her neck with a double chin,[1] and her cheeks with jewels and brilliants. He has also given her eyes which inspire love, and lashes sharp as polished blades. With admirable flanks and a delightful navel He has heightened the beauty of her gently domed belly. He has endowed her with buttocks nobly planned, and has supported the whole on majestic thighs. Between these latter He has placed the field of strife which, when it abounds in flesh, resembles by its amplitude a lion's head. Its name among mankind is 'vulva'.[2] Oh, how innumerable are the men who have died for this! how many, alas, of the bravest!

God has given this object a mouth, a tongue, two lips and a shape like unto the footprint of a gazelle on the sands of the desert.

All this is supported by two wonderful columns, witnesses to the power and wisdom of God; they are neither too long nor too short, and are ornamented with knees and calves, and ankles on which jewels repose. The Almighty has plunged woman into a sea of splendour, voluptuousness and delight; he has clothed her in precious raiment, and brightened her face with smiles.

Let praise be given to God that He has created woman with her beauty and appetizing flesh: that He has endowed her with hair, waist, and throat, breasts which swell, and amorous gestures which increase desire.

The Master of the Universe has given them a power of seduction over all men: weak or strong, without distinction, fall under the spell of their love. Communal life depends on women: it is they who decide for sojourn or dispersion.

The state of humility of the hearts of those who love but who are separated from the object of their affection; fires their breasts with the flames of love; it loads them with submissiveness, contempt and misery, and betrays them into all manner of vicissitudes as a consequence of their passion; and all that as the result of an ardent desire for union.

I, a servant of God, render thanks to Him that no man can withstand the charms of a beautiful woman, that no man can free himself from the desire of possession.

I testify that there is no other God but GOD himself, and that He has no partner! This testimony I carefully make in view of the Last Judgment.

I also bear witness to our Lord and Master MOHAMMED, the Servant of God and Lord of the Prophets (may the blessing and mercy of God be showered on him and his!) I reserve my prayers and benedictions for the day of retribution – God grant they be heard!

History of the present work

I have based this work on a small book dealing with the mysteries of generation, entitled 'The Torch of the Universe', which had been brought to the notice of the

1. The Arab ideal of feminine beauty was Rubenesque.

2. This medical-sounding term for the female sexual part is used throughout. Having adopted the rather charming 'yoni' for the Kama Sutra and Ananga-Ranga it is surprising that Burton did not annex a suitable word from Arabic: if he considered the vulgar 'kus' too strong, no-one had better knowledge of the many alternatives.

*'Her cheeks must be a perfect oval; she will have an elegant nose
and a graceful mouth; her lips will be vermilion. . . .'*

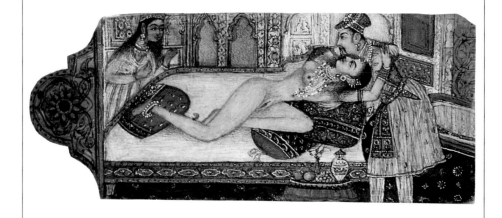

*A series of beautiful Mughal paintings on ivory depicting
the joys of physical love (above and page 116).*

Vizier of our Lord ABD EL AZIZ, master of Tunis, the well-protected. The illustrious Vizier was his poet, companion, friend, and private secretary. He was judicious, well-tried, sagacious and wise, the most learned of all the men of his time, and the one whose opinion was most often sought. His name was Mohammed ben Ouana ez Zouaoui, and he belonged to the tribe of the Zouaouas. He had been brought up at Algiers, and it was here that he made the acquaintance of our Lord Abd el Aziz el Hafsi. On the day of the Spanish conquest of Algiers (1510) our Lord fled with him to Tunis (may God in His might preserve him to the Resurrection Day!) and there elected him to the post of Grand Vizier.

When the afore-mentioned work came into his hands, he sent me a pressing invitation to visit him. I immediately went to his dwelling where he received me with the greatest kindness. Three days later he came to me and showed me my little book, and said:

'This is your work!'

Seeing that I blushed, he added:

'You have no cause for shame, for all you have written is quite true; there is nothing in it to frighten anyone. Besides, you are not the first to treat of these matters, and, I swear by God, the knowledge contained in this book should be widely known. It is only the ignorant and fearful who will avoid it or try to turn it to ridicule. But there are still a few things you ought to say.'

I asked him what they were.

'Oh, master!' I replied, 'all that you ask will be easy to perform if the work find favour in the sight of God.'

I immediately set to work to compile the treatise, imploring the aid of God (may He shower His blessings on His prophet, and grant us salvation and mercy!)

I have entitled my book The Perfumed Garden for the Repose of the Mind.

And I asked God who has arranged everything for our good (and there is only one God, and all good things come from Him!) to aid me with His support and to lead me into the right pathway. Our strength and happiness rest in God, the Almighty and All-highest!

Concerning Praiseworthy Men

Learn, Oh Vizier (may the blessing of God rest on you), that men and women are of divers kinds; some there are who are worthy of praise, while others deserve only censure.

When a worthy man is in the company of women his member grows, becomes strong, vigorous and hard; he is slow to ejaculate and, after the spasm caused by the emission of semen, he is prompt at re-erection.

Such a man is relished and appreciated by women, for they only love man for his sex. His member then must be well-developed: his chest should be light and his buttocks strong: he should be slow to ejaculate but quick to erect: his member should reach to the bottom of the vagina in which it should be a snug fit.

A man so endowed will be dearly cherished.

Qualities which Women look for in Men

It is related that on a certain day Abd el Melik ben Merouan sought out his mistress

Leilla and asked her questions concerning many things. Among others he asked her what qualities a woman looks for in a man.

She answered:

'Oh, master, they must have cheeks like ours.'

'And what else?'

'Hair like ours; in fact they must resemble thee, oh Prince of Believers; for verily if a man be not rich and powerful he will have no success with women.'

Concerning the length of the virile member

For a virile member to be pleasing to a woman its length should be, at most, three hand-breadths, and, at least, one hand-breadth and a half.[3] The man whose member is less than two-breadths long will enjoy but indifferent success.

3. The approximate nature of these measurements in early erotology is a point which has already been made: the Hindu tendency was towards understatement but the reader is reminded that hyperbole is indispensable to Arab writers.

On the utility of scents in coition

The story of Mosailama[4]

Scents have the power of exciting sexual desires in both man and woman. When a woman inhales the scent with which a man is perfumed she loses her power of control, and it will often be found that man has here a powerful means of gaining possession of a woman.

4. The device of an illustrative story, a kind of rambling secular parable, is typically Arab.

Touching this matter, it is related that Mosailama the imposter, son of Kais (whom God curse!) claimed to have the gift of prophecy, and that he imitated the Prophet of God (may blessings and salvation rest upon him!) On this account he and a great number of Arabs have incurred the anger of the Almighty.

Mosailama falsified the Koran by his lies and impostures, and, touching the chapter of the Koran which the angel Gabriel (God grant him salvation!) brought to the Prophet (the mercy of God be with him!) it is said that when some evil men came to Mosailama, he said to them: 'The angel Gabriel brought me a similar chapter.'

Now learn what happened to that woman of the Beni-Temim whose name was Sheja et Temimia and who claimed to prophesy: she had heard speak of Mosailama and he had heard speak of her.

This woman was powerful, for the Beni-Temim were a numerous tribe. She said: 'It is not meet that two persons should prophesy. Either he must be prophet and then I and my disciples will follow his laws, or I must be prophet and he and his disciples must follow mine.'

This happened after the death of the True Prophet, (on whom be the blessing of God!)

Sheja then wrote to Mosailama the following letter: It is not meet that two persons should prophesy simultaneously, but only one; we will meet and examine our doctrines, we and our disciples. We will discuss that which God has revealed to us, and we will follow the laws of the one who is judged to be the true prophet.

She then closed the letter and gave it to a courier, saying, 'Take this message to el Yamama and give it to Mosailama ben Kais; meanwhile, I will follow with my army.'

The next day the prophetess mounted her horse and, accompanied by her suite, followed in the steps of her envoy. When the latter reached Mosailama he greeted him and presented the letter.

Mosailama opened it, read it, and grasped its import; he was dismayed by the

'For a man to be successful with women he must pay
them marked attention. . . .'

'Do not unite with a woman until you have excited her with
playful caresses, and then the pleasure will be mutual.'

message and immediately took counsel of his suite, but they were unable to advise him. While he was thus perplexed one of his chief followers approached him and said:

'Oh, Mosailama, calm your mind and refresh your eyes. I am going to advise you as a father would a son.'

'Speak, and let your words be sincere,' replied Mosailama.

'Tomorrow morning let a tent of coloured brocade be raised on the outskirts of the town, and let it be richly furnished. Fill it then with delicious perfumes of various kinds, amber, musk, and scented flowers such as the rose, orange-blossom, jonquil, jasmine, hyacinth, pink, and others similar. That done, you will place in the tent golden cassolettes filled with perfumes, such as green aloes, ambergris, nedde, and other pleasant odours. Then the tent must be closed that none of the perfume can escape, and when the vapours have become sufficiently intense to impregnate the water which is in the tent, you will mount your throne and send for the prophetess, who will remain in the tent with you alone. When she inhales the perfumes she will be delighted, all her joints will slacken and she will swoon away. After having possessed her you will be spared further trouble from her.'

'Your advice is good,' exclaimed Mosailama. 'By God! it's a fine idea!'

He then took steps to put the plan in practice. As soon as he saw that the vapours were intense enough to impregnate the water in the tent, he mounted his throne and sent for the prophetess. When he saw her drawing near he ordered her to be shown into the tent. She entered and, when they were alone, he spoke to her. While he was

The setting is idyllic but we fear for the safety of these lovers, and marvel at them progressing so far.

speaking she began to lose her presence of mind; she seemed thunderstruck and stupefied.

When he saw her in this state he knew that she desired coition, so he said:

'Get up, so that I may possess you, for this place has been prepared for that purpose. If you desire it you may lie on your back, go on all fours, or take up the position used in prayer, with your head on the ground and your buttocks in the air like a tripod. Whatever posture you prefer, speak, and you shall be satisfied.'

'I want it all ways,' replied the prophetess. 'Let the revelation of God enter within me, oh Prophet of the Almighty!'

He at once fell upon her and enjoyed her as he would, after which she said:

'When I go out from here, ask me in marriage of my suite.'

She then left the tent and went to her disciples who asked her the result of the conference. She replied:

'Mosailama has shown me all that has been revealed to him, and I know it to be the truth: obey him!'

Mosailama asked her in marriage and the request was granted. When the disciples asked him about the future bride's dowry, he replied:

'I exempt you from saying the afternoon prayer.'

When the Beni-Temim are now asked why they do not say this prayer, they reply:

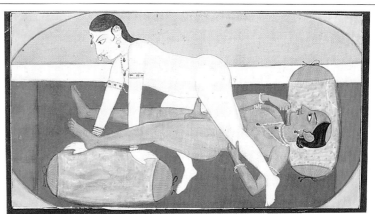

'Try different methods of copulating with your mistress and see which gives her most pleasure.'

'Because of our prophetess; she alone knows the way of truth.' And verily they acknowledge no other prophet but she.

The death of Mosailama was announced by the prophecy of Abou Beker (may God favour him!) He was, in fact, killed by Zeidben Khettab; others say by Ouhsha, one of his disciples.

As to Sheja, she repented and became a Musselman. Later she married a follower of the Prophet (may the Lord look with favour on her husband!)

Thus ends the story.

For a man to be successful with women he must pay them marked attention. His dress should be neat, his figure graceful, and his looks should mark him out from his fellows. He must be truthful and sincere, generous and brave. He should not be vain, and he should make himself agreeable in company. He must be the slave of his word; if he makes a promise he must keep it; he must always speak the truth and never fail to perform whatever he undertakes. He who boasts of his relations with women is contemptible.

Concerning Praiseworthy Women

Know, oh Vizier (may the blessing of God be upon you!) that there are women of divers kinds, some worthy of praise, others beneath contempt.

For a woman to be relished by man she must have a fine figure well endowed with flesh. Her hair should be black, her forehead wide; her brows should have the blackness of the Ethiopian's; her eyes should be big and black with pure whites. Her cheeks must be a perfect oval; she will have an elegant nose and a graceful mouth; her lips will be vermilion, as also her tongue; her breath will be agreeable, and her neck long and shapely; her bust and hips will be wide; her breasts must be firm and fill her chest; her belly must be well-proportioned and her navel developed and sunken; her vulva should be prominent and rich in flesh from the pubes to the buttocks; the passage must be narrow, free from humidity, soft to the touch and warm; her thighs must be hard, as also her buttocks; her waist must be slender; her hands and feet will be noticeable for their elegance; her arms will be plump, and her shoulders strong. If a woman possessing these qualities is seen from before, the sight is ravishing; if from behind, fatal. Viewed sitting, she is a rounded dome; lying, a downy bed; standing, she is as a flag-staff. When she walks her natural parts stand out under her clothing. She seldom speaks or laughs, and never without reason. She never leaves the house even to visit her neighbours. She has no woman-friend. She confides in no-one, and her husband is her sole support. She accepts no gifts but from her husband or his relations. If any of his relations are in the house she does not interfere with their business. She is not treacherous and has no faults to hide. She irritates nobody. If her husband intimates that he wishes to fulfil his conjugal duty she conforms to his desires and at times anticipates them. She always helps him in his business; she is sparing with complaints and tears; she does not laugh if she sees that her husband is downcast or sad, but she shares his troubles and fondles him till they have vanished, and she has no rest until she sees him content. She gives herself to none but her husband even though her abstinence may cause her death. She hides her secret parts from sight, observes the greatest cleanliness, and hides from her husband anything which might be repugnant to him. She perfumes herself and cleans her teeth with walnut bark.

Such a wife should be cherished by all men.

'Love's Bond . . . is the best movement of all . . . Tribads (lesbians) use no other movement.'

Concerning the Generative Act

Know, oh Vizier (may God protect you!) that, when you desire to copulate, let it be when your stomach is free from food. Only then is coition healthful and good. But if your stomach is loaded, the result will be bad for both persons; you will be liable to an attack of apoplexy and gout, and the least of the ills likely to afflict you will be either a stoppage of the urine or a weakness of sight. Let your stomach be free from all excess of food and drink and you will have nothing to fear.

Do not unite with a woman until you have excited her with playful caresses and then the pleasure will be mutual.

It is advisable therefore to amuse yourselves before you introduce your member and accomplish the act. You will excite her by kissing her cheeks, sucking her lips, and nibbling her teats. You will kiss her navel and thighs, and lay a provoking hand upon her pubes. Bite her arms; do not neglect any part of her body; clasp her tightly till she feels your love; then sigh and twine your arms and legs round hers.

When you are with a woman and you see that her eyes languish and she sighs profoundly, in a word, when she desires to copulate, let your two passions blend and your lubricity be carried to the highest point; for, so far as enjoyment is concerned, the favourable moment has arrived. The woman will then experience the supremest pleasure; you yourself will love her more and she will cling to you. It has been well

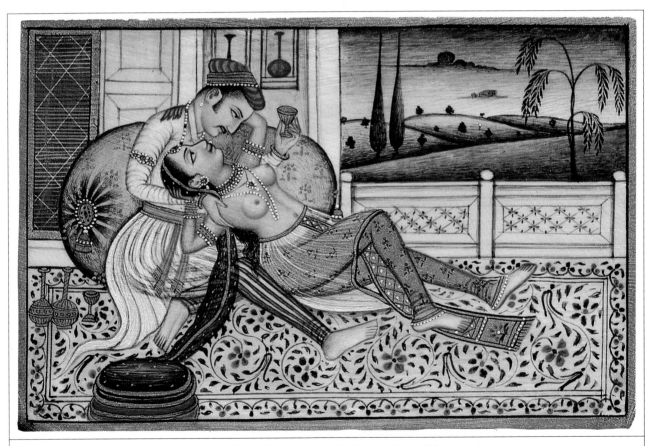

'No-one is insensible to the pleasures which arise from difference of sex,
and man's highest pleasure is copulation.'

*'Woman is no more satisfied than man with caresses
unfollowed by copulation.'*

said that: 'When you hear a woman sighing profoundly, and see her lips and ears become red and her eyes languishing, her mouth become slack and her movements slow; when she seems as if inclined for sleep and frequently yawns, know that this is the right moment for coition. If you penetrate her now her pleasure will be supreme, and you will certainly awaken the sucking power[5] of her vagina, which yields, without any doubt, the highest pleasure for both, and is the best guarantee that love will endure.

The following precepts were given by a student of the art of love: 'Woman is like a fruit which will only yield its fragrance when rubbed by the hands. Take, for example, the basil: unless it be warmed by the fingers it emits no perfume. And do you not know that unless amber be warmed and manipulated it retains its aroma within? The same with woman: if you do not animate her with your frolics and kisses, with nibbling of her thighs and close embraces, you will not obtain what you desire; you will experience no pleasure when she shares your couch, and she will feel no affection for you.

It is related that a man, having questioned a woman as to the things most likely to inspire affection for a man, received the following answer: 'The things which develop love for the moment of coition are the playful frolics practised in advance, and the

5. 'Jadeba', here translated 'sucking power', occurs several times in the text. It will henceforth be translated 'sucker' (Burton).

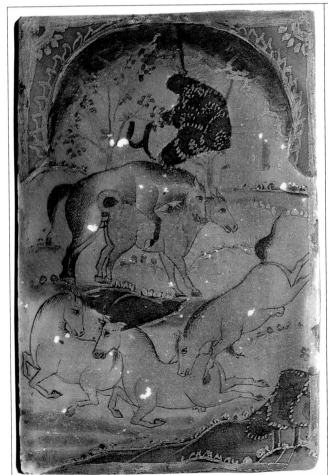

The sexual behaviour of animals was studied with interest by Sheikh Nefzawi.

vigorous embrace at the moment of ejaculation. Believe me, kisses, nibblings, sucking of lips, close-clasping of breasts, and the drinking of passion-loaded spittle, are the things which ensure a durable affection. Acting thus, the two ejaculations occur simultaneously, and enjoyment is complete for both. Add to that, the sucker will be brought into action, and no higher pleasure can be conceived. If things do not happen so, the woman's pleasure is incomplete and, if her desires are not satisfied and her sucker wakened to action, she will feel no love for her partner; but when the sucker is in action, she will have the most violent love for her lover, even though he be the ugliest man on earth. Try then by all means to make the ejaculations simultaneous, for that is the secret of love.'

One of the cleverest men who have made a study of women relates the following feminine confidence: 'Oh, you men who seek for the love and affection of women and desire to retain them, see that you frolic before copulation. Prepare her for the enjoyment and let nothing be neglected to attain this end. Explore her with all possible activity and, while so doing, let your mind be free from all other thought. Do not let pleasure's propitious moment pass by unheeded: it occurs when you see her eyes slightly moist and her mouth partly open. Unite, then, but never before. Therefore, oh men, when you have brought woman to the favourable condition, introduce your

*Islamic erotology (above and opposite) was generally more concerned
with medical matters than the Hindu tradition.*

127

member; then if you take care to move in the proper manner, she will experience a pleasure which will satisfy all her desires. Do not rise yet from her breast, but let your lips wander over her cheeks, and let your sword rest in her sheath. Seek ardently to arouse her sucker, so will your work be worthily crowned. If by the favour of the All-highest you achieve success, be careful not to withdraw your member, but let it remain and drain the cup of pleasure. Give ear and listen to the sighs and cries and murmurs of the woman, for these bear witness to the violence of the pleasure you have procured her.

And when the cessation of enjoyment puts an end to your amorous frolics, take care not to rise brusquely, but withdraw your member with circumspection; stay with the woman, lying on your right side in this bed of pleasure. In this way nothing but good will result, and you will not be like those who mount a woman as a mule would, paying no attention to the principles of the art, and who withdraw and hurry away as soon as they have ejaculated. So crude a method must be avoided as it deprives the woman of all pleasure.'

To sum up, it behoves the connoisseur of copulation to omit none of my recommendations, for it is on the observance of these that woman's happiness depends.

Concerning all that is Favourable to Coition

Know, oh Vizier, (God's mercy be with you!) that if you wish to experience an agreeable copulation, one that gives equal satisfaction and pleasure to both parties, it is necessary to frolic with the woman and excite her with nibbling, kissing, and caressing. Turn her over on the bed, sometimes on her back, sometimes on her belly, until you see by her eyes that the moment of pleasure has arrived, as I have described in the previous chapter, and, on my honour! I have not stinted the descriptions.

When, therefore, you see a woman's lips tremble and redden, and her eyes become languishing and her sighs profound, know that she desires coition; then is the time to get between her thighs and penetrate her. If you have followed my advice you will both enjoy a delightful copulation which will leave a delicious memory. Someone has said: 'If you desire to copulate, place the woman on the ground, embrace her closely and put your lips on hers; then clasp her, suck her, bite her; kiss her neck, her breasts, her belly and her flanks; strain her to you until she lies limp with desire. When you see her in this state, introduce your member. If you act thus your enjoyment will be simultaneous, and that is the secret of pleasure. But if you neglect this plan the woman will not satisfy your desires, and she herself will gain no enjoyment.'

When the act is finished and you wish to rise, do not do so suddenly, but withdraw gently from her right side and, if she has conceived, she will bear a son—if God will have it so! It has been said by some wise man (may God pardon him!) that if someone puts his hand on a pregnant woman's vulva and says: 'In the name of God! let His mercy be with His Prophet! Oh God, I pray You, in the name of the Prophet, let this be a boy,' it may happen that by the will of God and in consideration of our Lord Mohammed, (on whom be God's mercy!) the woman will bear a boy.

Do not drink rain-water immediately after coition as it tends to weaken the loins.

If you wish to repeat the act, perfume yourself with sweet odours, then approach the woman, and you will attain a happy result.

It is advisable to rest after coition and not indulge in any violent exercise.

The Mughal artist who painted these luscious harem women
had a way with flesh tones reminiscent of Vargas.

Concerning the Different Postures for Coition

The ways of uniting with a woman are numerous and varied, and the time has arrived when you should learn the different postures. God has said: 'Woman is your field, go to your field with a will!' (Koran).

According to your taste you may choose the posture which pleases you most, provided always that intercourse takes place through the appointed organ: the vulva.

First posture Lay the woman on her back and raise her thighs; then, getting between her legs, introduce your member. Gripping the ground with your toes, you will be able to move in a suitable manner. This posture is a good one for those who have long members.

Second posture If your member is short, lay the woman on her back and raise her legs in the air so that her toes touch her ears. Her buttocks being thus raised, the vulva is thrown forward. Now introduce your member.

Third posture Lay the woman on the ground and get between her thighs; then, putting one of her legs on your shoulder and the other under your arm, penetrate her.

Fourth posture Stretch the woman on the ground and put her legs on your shoulders; in that position your member will be exactly opposite her vulva which will be lifted off the ground. That is the moment for introducing your member.

Fifth posture Let the woman lie on her side on the ground; then, lying down yourself and getting between her thighs, introduce your member. This posture is apt to give rise to rheumatic or sciatic pains.[6]

Sixth posture Let the woman rest on her knees and elbows in the position for prayer. In this posture the vulva stands out behind. Attack her thus.

Seventh posture Lay the woman on her side, and then you yourself sitting on your heels will place her top leg on your nearest shoulder and her other leg against your thighs. She will keep on her side and you will be between her legs. Introduce your member and move her backwards and forwards with your hands.

Eighth posture Lay the woman on her back and kneel astride her.

Ninth posture Place the woman so that she rests, either face forward or the reverse, against a slightly raised platform, her feet remaining on the ground and her body projecting in front. She will thus present her vulva to your member which you will introduce.

Tenth posture Place the woman on a rather low divan and let her grasp the woodwork with her hands; then, placing her legs on your hips and telling her to grip your body with them, you will introduce your member, at the same time grasping the divan. When you begin to work, let your movements keep time.

Eleventh posture Lay the woman on her back and let her buttocks be raised by a cushion placed under them. Let her put the soles of her feet together: now get between her thighs.

There are other postures besides the preceding in use in India.[7] It is well that you should know that the Hindus have greatly multiplied the ways of possessing a woman and have carried their investigations in this matter much farther than the Arabs. Among other postures and variations are the following:

The closure Lay the woman on her back and raise her buttocks with a cushion; then get between her legs, keeping your toes on the floor, and force her thighs against her chest. Now pass your hands under her arms to clasp her to you, or tightly grip her shoulders. That done, introduce your member and draw her towards you at the moment of ejaculation. This posture is painful for the woman, for, with her thighs pressed on her chest and her buttocks raised with the cushion, the walls of the vagina

6. Sheikh Nefzawi's patron, the Vizier Mohammed ben Ouana ez Zouaoui, had a particular interest in medical matters, and these snippets of ostensible erudition have all the signs of journalistic confection.

7. In the explosion of energy released by The Prophet, conquering Arab armies changed the face of the known world. Less than a century after Mohammed's death in A.D. 632 the first Indian conquest was made in Sind. At the time The Perfumed Garden was written, Islamic domination was complete and cultural and scientific exchange between Arab countries commonplace.

*'A robust temperament is indispensable for copulation and he
who is so endowed can indulge without danger.'*

are forced together, and, as a consequence—the uterus being pushed forward—there is not enough room for the penis which can only be inserted with difficulty, and which impinges on the womb. This posture should only be used when the penis is short and soft.

The frog's posture Place the woman on her back and raise her thighs till her heels are close to her buttocks. Now seat yourself in front of her vulva and introduce your member; then put her knees under your armpits and, grasping the upper part of her arms, draw her to you at the propitious moment.

The clasping of hands and feet Lay the woman on her back, then sit on your heels between her thighs and grip the floor with your toes; she will now put her legs round your body and you will put your arms about her neck.

The raised legs posture While the woman is lying on her back take hold of her legs and, holding them close together, raise them until her soles point to the ceiling; then clasping her between your thighs, introduce your member, taking care at the same time not to let her legs fall.

The goat's posture Let the woman lie on her side and stretch out the bottom leg. Crouch down between her thighs, lift her top leg and introduce your member. Hold her by the arms or shoulders.

The Archimedean screw[8] While the man is lying on his back the woman sits on his member, keeping her face towards his. She then places her hands on the bed, at the same time keeping her belly off his; she now moves up and down and, if the man is

8. Islam had absorbed all the scientific knowledge of the Classical World and such a title for a sexual position is possible although more likely to owe its invention to Burton's humour.

'Know that a prudent man will not abuse the pleasure of copulation.'

light in weight, he may move as well. If the woman wishes to kiss the man she need only lay her arms on the bed.

The stab with a lance[9] Suspend the woman face upwards from the ceiling by means of four cords attached to her hands and feet and another supporting the middle of her body. Her position should be such that her vulva is now opposite your member, you standing up. Introduce your member and then begin to swing her, first away from you, then towards you. You thus alternately introduce and withdraw your member, and so you continue until you ejaculate.

The hanging posture The woman lies face downwards, and the man fixes cords to her hands and feet and raises her by means of a pulley fixed to the ceiling. He then lies under her, holds the other end of the rope in his hand, and lets her down so that he can penetrate her. He raises and lowers her until he ejaculates.

The summersault The woman should let her trousers fall to her ankles so that they are like fetters. She then bends down till her head is in her trousers, when the man, seizing her legs, pulls her over onto her back. He then kneels down and penetrates her. It is said that there are women, who, when lying on their back, can put their feet under their head without the help of their hands or trousers.

The ostrich's tail Lay the woman on the ground and kneel at her feet; then raise her legs and place them round your neck so that only her head and shoulders remain on the ground. Now penetrate her.

Putting on the sock The woman being on her back, you sit between her legs and place

9. This and the next posture are denied to all but skilled acrobats with access to a private gymnasium: definitely not to be taken seriously!

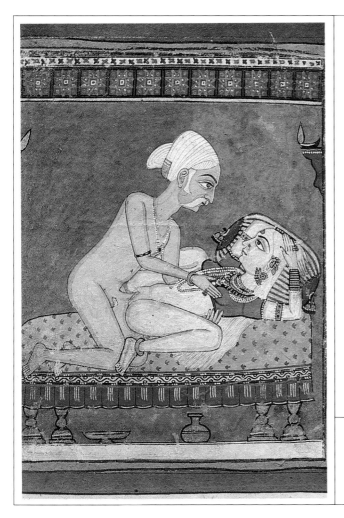

Sheikh Nefzawi describes this as 'the seductive posture.'

'Avoid remaining with the woman after you have ejaculated . . . it tends to turn the hair grey': a 'fact' long-suppressed by makers of hair restorative.

your member between the lips of her vulva which you grasp with the thumb and first finger. You then move so that the part of your member which is in contact with the woman is subjected to rubbing, and continue so until her vulva is moist with the liquid which escapes from your penis. Having thus given her a foretaste of pleasure, you penetrate her completely.

The mutual view of the buttocks The man lies on his back, and the woman, turning her back to him, sits on his member. He now clasps her body with his legs and she leans over until her hands touch the floor. Thus supported she has a view of his buttocks, and he of hers, and she is able to move conveniently.

Drawing the bow Let the woman lie on her side, and the man, also on his side, get between her legs so that his face is turned towards her back; now, placing his hands on her shoulders, he introduces his member. The woman then grasps the man's feet and draws them towards her; she forms thus, with the man's body, a bow to which she is the arrow.

Reciprocating motion The man, seated on the ground, brings the soles of his feet together, at the same time lowering his thighs. The woman then sits on his feet and clasps his body with her legs and his neck with her arms. The man then grasps the woman's legs, and, moving his feet towards his body, carries the woman within reach of his member, which he introduces. By a movement of his feet he now moves her backwards and forwards. The woman should take care to facilitate this movement by not pressing too heavily. If the man fears that his member will be drawn right out, he must grasp the woman round the body and be satisfied with such movement as he can give with his feet.

Pounding the spot The man sits down and stretches out his legs, and the woman sits on his thighs and crosses her legs behind his back. She places her vulva opposite his penis and lends a guiding hand. She then puts her arms round his neck, and he puts his round her waist and raises and lowers her on his member, in which movement she assists.

Coition from behind The woman lies face downwards and raises her buttocks with a cushion; the man lies on her back and introduces his member while she slips her arms through his elbows.

Belly to belly The man and the woman stand face to face, the latter with her feet slightly apart, the man's feet being between. Both now advance their feet. The man should now place one foot in advance of the other, and each should clasp the other round the loins. The man then penetrates and both move in the manner explained later on. (See first movement.)

The sheep's posture The woman kneels down and puts her fore-arms on the ground; the man kneels down behind her and slips his penis in her vulva which she makes stand out as much as possible. His hands should be placed on her shoulders.

The camel's hump The woman, who is standing, bends forward till her fingers touch the floor; the man gets behind and copulates, at the same time grasping her thighs. If the man withdraws while the woman is still bending down, the vagina emits a sound like the bleating of a calf, and for that reason women object to the posture.

Driving in the peg While facing each other, the woman, hanging with her arms round the man's neck, raises her legs and with them clasps him round the waist, resting her feet against a wall. The man now introduces his member, and the woman is then as if hanging on a peg.[10]

The fusion of love The woman lies on her right side and you on your left; stretch your bottom leg straight down and raise your other leg, letting it rest on the woman's side. Now pull the woman's top leg onto your body and then introduce your member. The woman may help if she likes, to make the necessary movements.

Coition by violence The man goes up behind the woman and takes her by surprise. He

10. All standing postures where the man takes the woman's weight are to be attempted with great caution. If the couple slip, and weight is taken on the erect penis, it can be permanently damaged.

*'He who makes love to satisfy his mistress . . . imperils his
well-being merely to give pleasure to another.'*

'Let praise be given to God that he has created woman. . . .'

thrusts his hands below her armpits and onto the back of her neck, at the same time forcing her head down. If she is not wearing trousers he will try to lift her dress with his knees, and preventing her from moving her legs by pressing against them so that she cannot turn and so prevent the introduction of his member. But, if she is strong and wearing trousers, he will be obliged to hold both her hands with one of his, and, with the other, pull her garment down.

Inversion The man lies on his back and the woman lies on him. She grasps his thighs and draws them towards her, thus bringing his member into prominence. Having guided it in, she puts her hands on the bed, one on each side of the man's buttocks. It is necessary for her feet to be raised on a cushion to allow for the slope of the penis. The woman moves.

This posture may be varied by the woman sitting on her heels between the man's legs.

Riding the member The man lies down and places a cushion under his shoulders, taking care that his buttocks remain on the floor. Thus placed, he raises his legs till his knees are close to his face. The woman then sits on his member. She does not lie down, but sits astride, as though on a saddle formed by the man's legs and chest. By bending her knees she can now move upwards and downwards; or, she may put her knees on the floor, in which case the man moves her with his thighs while she grasps his shoulders.

The jointer The man and the woman sit down facing each other; the woman then puts her right thigh on the man's left thigh, and he puts his right thigh on her left one. The woman guides his member into her vagina and grasps the man's arms while he grasps hers. They now indulge in a see-saw motion, leaning backwards and forwards alternately, taking care that their movements are well-timed.

The stay-at-home The woman lies on her back, and the man, with cushions under his hands, lies on her. When the introduction has taken place the woman raises her buttocks as far as possible from the bed, and the man accompanies her in the movement, taking care that his member is not withdrawn. The woman then drops her buttocks with short sharp jerks, and, although the two are not clasped together, the man should keep quite close to the woman. They continue this movement, but it is necessary that the man be light and the bed soft; otherwise pain will be caused.

The blacksmith's posture The woman lies on her back with a cushion under her buttocks. She now draws her knees onto her chest so that her vulva stands out like a sieve; she then guides in the member. The man now performs for a moment or two the conventional movements. He then withdraws his member and slips it between the women's thighs in imitation of the blacksmith who draws the hot iron from the fire and plunges it into cold water.

The seductive posture The woman lies on her back and the man crouches between her legs which he then puts under his arms or on his shoulders. He may hold her by the waist or the arms.

The preceding descriptions furnish a greater number of postures than can generally be made use of; but the large number will enable those who experience any difficulty in practising some of them to find which suit them the best and give them most pleasure.

I have not thought it necessary to mention those postures which appeared to me impossible of accomplishment and, if anyone should think the number given is too small, he has nothing to do but invent more.

It is incontestable that the Hindus have surmounted enormous difficulties in postures for coition; the following is an example:

The woman lies on her back and the man sits astride her chest, facing towards her feet. He now bends forward and raises her thighs till her vulva is opposite his member which he then introduces.

As you can see, this posture is difficult to execute and very tiring. I think it is only realizable in thought or design.

It is related that there are women who, during coition, can raise one of their legs in the air and balance a lighted lamp on the sole of their foot, without spilling the oil or extinguishing the lamp. Intercourse is not interfered with by this action which demands, however, great skill.

Nevertheless, the things to be sought for most in copulation, those which give the greatest pleasure, are the embraces, the kisses, and the sucking of each other's lips. These differentiate man from the animals. No-one is insensible to the pleasures which arise from difference of sex, and man's highest pleasure is copulation.

When a man's love is carried to its highest pitch, all the pleasures of coition become easy for him, and he satisfies them by embracing and kissing. There is the real source of happiness for both.

It is advisable that the connoisseur of copulation should try all the postures so that he may know which gives pleasure to the woman. He will then adopt that for preference and will have the satisfaction of retaining the woman's affection. By universal consent, the fifteenth posture (pounding on the spot) gives most satisfaction.

It is related that a man had a mistress of incomparable beauty, grace, and perfection. He was in the habit of copulating with her in the ordinary way to the exclusion of any other. The woman experienced none of the pleasure which should accompany the act, and was always ill-tempered afterwards. The man told his trouble to an old woman, who said: 'Try different methods of copulating with your mistress and see which gives her most pleasure. When you have found it, never use another, and she will love you without bounds.'

So the man tried various postures, and when he came to the one called Pounding on the Spot, he saw that the woman's pleasure was intense, and felt his member powerfully seized. The woman exclaimed, while biting his lips: 'That's the proper way to make love!'

These demonstrations proved to the lover that his mistress experienced the greatest pleasure from this posture, so he never used another.

Try, then, the different postures, for every woman prefers the one which gives her the greatest pleasure; but the majority show a marked predilection for the one before-mentioned, for, in practising it, belly is pressed against belly, and mouth on mouth, and rarely does the sucker fail to act.

It remains now for me to speak of the different movements used in copulation. First movement. *The bucket in the well* The man and woman embrace closely after penetration, then the man moves once and slightly draws back; the woman now moves and withdraws in her turn, and so on alternately. They should take care to place their hands and feet against each others and imitate, as well as they can, the descent of a bucket in a well.

Second movement. *The mutual shock* Both draw away after the introduction, taking care that the member is not entirely withdrawn; they then come together smartly and closely embrace. They contine thus.

Third movement. *Going shares* The man moves in the usual manner, then stops; the woman, keeping the member in place, moves once, then stops. The man now recommences, and so they continue till they ejaculate.

Fourth movement. *Love's tailor* The man partly penetrates and moves with a rubbing motion; then, with a single stroke, he enters completely. Such is the action of a tailor who, after having inserted his needle, draws it through with a single pull. This

'God has said, "Woman is your field, go to your field as you will!"'

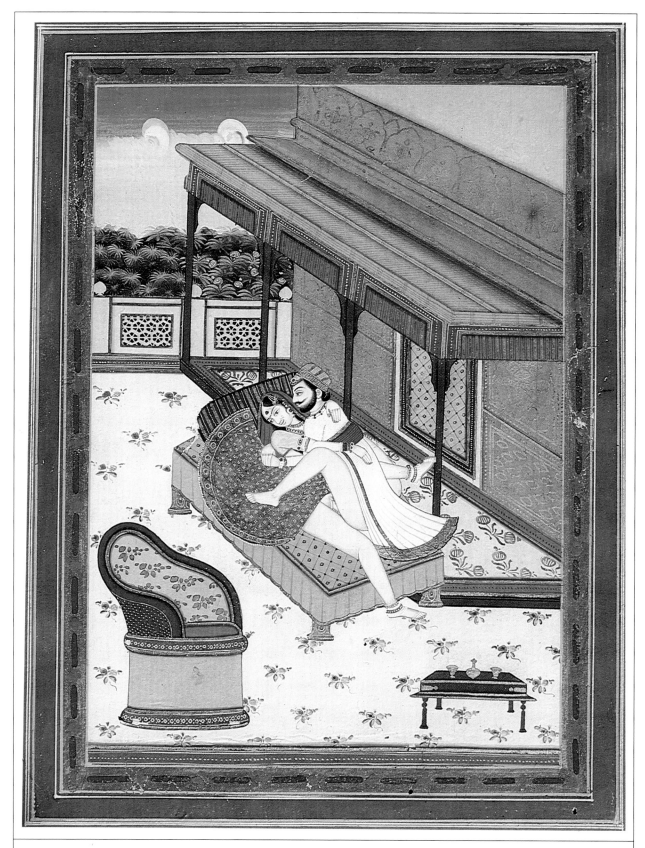

*'When, therefore, you see a woman's lips tremble and redden
. . . know that she desires coition.'*

movement is only suitable for those who can control their ejaculation.

Fifth movement. *The tooth-pick* The man introduces his member and explores the vagina from top to bottom and on all sides. This movement requires a vigorous instrument.

Sixth movement. *Love's bond* The man penetrates completely so that his body is perfectly close to the woman's. He should now move energetically, taking care that not the smallest portion is withdrawn from the vulva.

This is the best movement of all, and it is particularly suitable for the fifteenth posture. Women prefer it to the exclusion of all others as it procures them the greatest pleasure, and allows the vagina to clasp the penis. Tribads use no other movement, and it can be recommended to all who suffer from a premature ejaculation.

Any posture is unsatisfactory if kissing is impossible; pleasure will be incomplete, for a kiss is one of the most potent stimulants that a man or woman can indulge in. For woman it is particularly so, especially if she is alone and sheltered from indiscreet regards.

It is claimed by some that kissing is an integral part of copulation.

The most delightful kiss is that which is planted on moist ardent lips, and accompanied with suction of the lips and tongue, so that the emission of a sweet intoxicating saliva is produced. It is for the man to procure this emission from the woman by gently nibbling her lips and tongue till she secretes a particular saliva, sweet, exquisite, more agreeable than honey mixed with pure water, and which does not mix with her ordinary saliva. This gives the man a shivering sensation throughout his whole body, and is more intoxicating than strong wine.

A kiss should be sonorous. Its sound, light and prolonged, takes its rise between the tongue and the moist edge of the palate. It is produced by a movement of the tongue in the mouth and a displacement of the saliva provoked by suction.

A kiss given on the outside of the lips and accompanied with a sound like that made when calling a cat, gives no pleasure whatever. Such a kiss is only meant for children, or the hands. The kiss which I have described above, and which belongs to copulation provokes a delicious voluptuousness. It is for you to learn the difference.

Know that all the kisses and caresses mentioned above are useless if unaccompanied by the introduction of the penis. You should therefore abstain if not able to copulate, or otherwise you light a fire which only a sterile separation can quench. Passion which inflames resembles a fire, and as only water can extinguish this, so only can semen extinguish the fires of love. Woman is no more satisfied than man with caresses unfollowed by copulation.

It is related that Dahama ben Mesejel complained before the governor of the province of Yahama that her husband, El Ajaje, was impotent and neither cohabited with her nor approached her. Her father, who assisted her in the case, was blamed by the people of Yamama for this, and they asked him if he was not ashamed to demand coition for his daughter.

'I want her to have some childern,' replied he; 'if she loses them, God will hold her to account; if she keeps them, they will be useful.'

Dahama presented her case in these words to the emir:
'Here is my husband; up to now he has left me intact.'

'You are perhaps unwilling,' objected the emir.

'On the contrary, I willingly lie down and open my legs.'

'Oh emir, she lies! If I want to possess her I have to fight hard,' exclaimed her husband.

'I will give you a year in which to prove the falsity of the allegation,' replied the emir to him. This he did, however, out of sympathy for the man.

El Ajaje then withdrew.

As soon as he got back home he took his wife in his arms and began to caress her and kiss her on the mouth; but that was the limit of his efforts, for he could give no proof of his virility. Dahama said to him: 'Cease your caresses and embraces; they do not suffice for love. What I need is a strong and rigid member whose sperm will flood my womb.'

In despair, Ajaje took her back to her family and repudiated her that very night.

Know then that if a woman is to be satisfied, kisses without coition will not suffice. Her sole delight is in the penis, and she gives her love to the man who can use it well, however disagreeable and deformed he is.

It is related that Moussa ben Mesab went one day to the house of a lady who owned a female slave, a beautiful singer, to see if he could buy her. Now this lady was a great beauty and very rich. When he entered the house he noticed a man, still young but very deformed, who was giving orders. He enquired of the lady who the man was, and she replied:
'That is my husband, and I would willingly die for him.'

'You are reduced to a hard slavery, and I pity you; but we belong to God and shall return to Him! Still, what a calamity that such incomparable beauty and such a figure should belong to that man!'

'Oh son, if he did to you behind what he does to me in front, you would sell all your goods and even your patrimony. You would then think him handsome, and his ugliness would change to perfection.'

'May God preserve him for you!' exclaimed Moussa.

Concerning the Divers Names of the Virile Member

Know, oh Vizier (God grant you mercy!), that the virile member had many names,[11] among which are the following:
The virile member — Generative organ — Smith's bellows — Pigeon — Jingler — Untameable — Liberator — Creeper — Exciter — Deceiver — Sleeper — Pathmaker — Tailor — Quencher — Twister — Knocker — Swimmer — Enterer — Withdrawer — One-eyed — Bald-head — One with an eye — Stumbler — Funny-head — One with a neck — Hairy one — Shameless one — Bashful one — Weeper — Mover — Annexer — Spitter — Splasher — Breaker — Seeker — Rubber — Flabby one — Searcher — Discoverer.

The first two names present no difficulty.
The smith's bellows It has received this name because of its alternative inflation and deflation.
The pigeon It is so called because, after having been swollen and at the moment when it is returning to its state of repose, it resembles a pigeon settling on its eggs.
The jingler It is so called on account of the noise it makes each time it enters or leaves the vulva.
The untameable It has received this name because, when it is swollen and erect, it starts to move its head, looking for the entrance to the vagina, which, when found, it brusquely and insolently enters.
The liberator So named because, when entering the vulva of a divorced woman, it frees her from the prohibition of remarrying her former husband.

11. Both author and translator evidently enjoyed compiling the listings in this and the next chapter. It is hard to imagine Vatsyayana and Kalyana Malla (Sherlock Holmes and Dr Watson, respectively) having as much fun with their subject.

'It behoves a connoisseur of copulation to omit none of my recommendations,
for it is on the observance of these that the woman's happiness depends.

The creeper This name has been given to the penis because, when it gets between a woman's thighs and sees a plump vulva, it starts to creep on her legs and pubis, then, approaching the entrance, it continues to creep until it has taken possession. When comfortably installed it penetrates completely and ejaculates.

The exciter It has received this name because it irritates the vulva with its repeated entrances and exits.

The deceiver It gets this name from its tricks and ruses. When it desires coition, it says: 'If God gives me the chance of meeting with a vulva, I will never quit it!' but, when it finds one, it is soon satisfied, its presumption becomes apparent and it throws a despairing look at the vulva, for it bragged that once inside it would never come out. At the approach of a woman it draws itself up and seems to say to the vulva: 'Today, oh my soul, I will quench my desires with you!', and the vulva, seeing it erect and stiff, is surprised at its size and seems to reply: 'Whoever could accommodate such a member?' Its only reply is to place its head at the door of the vulva, force open the lips and sink right in. When it starts to move the vulva makes fun of it and says: 'What a deceptive movement!' for he is no sooner in than out. The two testicles seem to say: 'Our friend is dead; he has succumbed after his pleasure, the quenching of his passion and the ejaculation of his sperm!' He then withdraws precipitately from the vulva and tries to hold up his head again, but he falls flabby and inert. The testicles repeat: 'Our brother is dead . . . our brother is dead!' He protests, saying: 'Why do you withdraw? Oh, liar, you said that when once you were in you would never come out.'

The sleeper This name is due to its deceptive appearance. When it enters in erection it lengthens and stiffens to such a pitch that you would never think it would soften again, but, when it leaves the vulva after slaking its passion, it falls asleep.

The pathmaker It has this name because, when it meets a vulva which will not let it enter at once, it makes a passage with its head, breaking and tearing all like a ruttish beast.

The tailor It gets this name from the fact that it does not enter the vulva until after it has manoeuvred at the entrance, like a needle in the hand of a tailor.

The quencher This name is given to a thick strong member which is slow to ejaculate. Such a member fully satisfies woman's amorous desires because, after having raised them to the highest pitch, it quenches them better than any other. When it wishes to enter a vulva and, on arriving at the entrance, finds it closed, it laments, pleads, and makes promises backed by pledges: 'Oh, dear friend, let me enter . . . I will not stay long'; but, when it has gained its cause, it breaks its word by prolonging its stay, and not withdrawing until after it has ejaculated and exhausted its ardour by dint of moving in and out, up and down, and right and left. The vulva demands: 'What about your promise, oh liar? You said you would only stay a moment!' But he replies: 'Oh, I shall not withdraw until I have met your womb, but I promise to do so then.' At these words the vulva is overcome with pity, it wakes the sucker which grips the member by the head and satisfies it completely.

The twister This name was given to it because it arrives at the vulva as if on urgent business. It knocks at the door, twists and turns about in a shameless manner, pushing its investigations to right and left, before and behind, then suddenly penetrating to the bottom of the vagina to ejaculate.

The knocker It is thus named because, when it arrives at the door of the vulva, it gives a light knock; if the vulva replies and opens the door, it enters; but, if it gets no reply, it knocks again until successful. By knocking at the door we refer to the rubbing of the penis on the vulva until it becomes moist. The production of this moisture is what is called opening the door.

The swimmer This is the one which, when it enters the vagina, does not remain in one

'Do not let pleasure's propitious moment pass by unheeded. . . .'

place but turns to right and left, before and behind, but principally in the middle, and swims about in the sperm which it ejects and the fluid secreted by the woman as if, fearing to be drowned, it struggles to save its life.

The enterer This merits its name because, when it arrives at the door of the vulva, this latter says: 'What is your wish?' and it replies: 'I wish to enter.' The vulva replies: 'That is impossible . . . I cannot receive you on account of your size.' The enterer then asks to be allowed to introduce its head, promising not to penetrate completely; it approaches the vulva, rubs its head two or three times between the lips until it has provoked the secretion, then, when the vulva is well lubricated, it takes a sudden plunge and buries itself completely.

The withdrawer So called because, when it approaches a vulva which has been deprived for a long time of coitus and which it wishes to enter, the vulva will say (influenced by the violence of its amorous desire): 'Yes, but on one condition . . . that, if you enter, you will not withdraw until you have ejaculated so many times!' The member replies: 'I promise not to withdraw until I have done it three times more than you ask.' Once entered, the intensity of the vulva's heat activates the enjoyment; it moves up and down, seeking the perfect pleasure which this movement procures by the alternate rubbings against the vulva and the womb. When the ejaculation takes place the member seeks to withdraw, which makes the vulva say: 'Oh, liar, why do you withdraw? You ought to be called the lying withdrawer.'

'Woman is like a fruit which will yield its fragrance only when rubbed by the hands.'

'Try then by all means to make the ejaculations simultaneous, for that is the secret of love.'

The one-eyed The force of this name is obvious.

The bald-head As above.

The one with an eye It has this name because its solitary eye presents this peculiarity, that it has neither pupils nor lashes.

The stumbler It has been so called because, when it wishes to enter the vulva and not seeing the door, it bumps above and below and continues so as if it were stumbling against a stone on the road, until the lips of the vulva are lubricated and it can enter. The vulva then asks: 'What made you stumble so? 'Oh, my friend, there was a stone in my way,' it replies.

The funny-head It has this name because its head is different from all others.

The one with a neck It is he whose neck is short and thick and big behind. Its head is skinned and the pubic hair is stubborn.

The hairy one This needs no explanation.

The shameless one It has received this name because, from the minute it gets stiff and long, it cares for nobody. It unblushingly lifts its master's raiment, caring nought for the shame he feels. It acts in the same shameless way with woman. It will lift her clothes and expose her thighs. Its master may feel shame at this conduct, but, as for itself, its stiffness and ardour go on increasing.

The bashful one This member, met with in some individuals, feels shame and becomes bashful when in the presence of an unknown vulva, and it is only after a time that it raises its head. Sometimes its trouble is so great that it remains quite impotent, especially if a stranger is near.

The weeper So called because of the many tears it sheds. As soon as it stands, it begins to weep; if it sees a pretty face, it weeps; if it touches a woman, it weeps. It even at times weeps tears of remembrance.

The mover So called because, as soon as it enters the vulva, it moves about till its ardour is quenched.

The annexer This gets its name because, when it enters the vulva, it starts to move, but, at the same time, clings closely hair to hair and even tries to force the testicles in.

The spitter It has received this name because, at the approach of the vulva or at its aspect, or even simply at its memory, or when its master touches a woman, plays with her or kisses her, its saliva begins to flow; this saliva is particularly abundant after a long abstinence and will sometimes soak the clothing. This member is very common and few are the men not so endowed.

The liquid thus poured out is known as the medi. A discharge may be caused by lascivious thoughts. It is so abundant with some men that it fills the vulva, so much so that many think it derives from the woman.

The splasher So called because it makes a splashing noise when it enters the vulva.

The breaker This is the vigorous member which gets long and stiff like a rod or a bone. It easily breaks through a maidenhead.

The seeker This name was given because, when it is in the vulva, it starts to move about as if it were looking for something. It is looking for the womb, and it has no peace till it finds it.

The rubber It gets this name because it does not enter the vagina until it has rubbed against the vulva several times. It is often confounded with the following.

The flabby one The one which can never penetrate because it is too soft and so must be content with rubbing against the vulva until it ejaculates. It gives no pleasure to a woman for it only enflames her passions and cannot quench them.

The searcher So called because it penetrates into unusual places, takes particulars of the state of vulvas, and knows how to distinguish their good and bad qualities.

The discoverer It has been so called because, when it gets stiff and holds up its head, it lifts the clothes which hide it and so betrays its master by uncovering his nudity; nor does it fear to expose the vulvas which are unknown to it by shamelessly lifting the women's garments. It is quite inaccessible to any feeling of shame and has no respect for anyone. Nothing relative to coition is unknown to it. It has a profound knowledge of the humidity, freshness, dryness, narrowness, or heat of vulvas, the insides of which are well-known to it. There are some vulvas which are externally perfect, plump and good-looking, while their interior is far from satisfactory. They give no pleasure because of their excessive moisture or their lack of warmth. It is because this member sets out to find all that can add to the pleasure of coition that it has received its name.

Such are the principal names which have been given to the virile member, corresponding to its distinguishing qualities. It is lawful for those who find the list insufficient to look for others, but I limit myself there as the names given will satisfy most of my readers.

Concerning the Female Organs

The following are the usual names:−
The passage − Vulva − Libidinous − Primitive − Starling − Crack − Crested One − Snub-nosed − Hedgehog − Taciturn − Squeezer − Importunate − Sprinkler − Desirer − Beauty − Sweller − High-brow − Spreader − Giant − Glutton − Bottomless pit − Two-lipped one − Camel's hump − Sieve − Mover − Annexer − Accommodator − Helper − Arch − Extender − Duellist − Ever-ready − Fleer − Resigned − Wet one − Barricaded one − Abyss − Biter − Sucker − Wasp − Warmer − Delicious one

The passage It has received this name (el feuj) because it opens and closes like the vulva of a mare in heat.
The vulva Such an organ is plump and outstanding in its full length; the lips are long, the opening large, the edges apart and perfectly symmetrical, and the middle prominent; it is soft, seductive, and perfect in all its details. It is, without fear of contradiction, the most agreeable and the best of all. May God grant us the use of such a vulva! Amen! It is warm, narrow and dry to such a degree that one would think fire would dart from it. Its form is graceful, its odour suave; its whiteness throws the carmine centre into relief. In a word, it is perfect.
The libidinous A name given to a virgin's vulva.
The primitive This name is applicable to any vulva.
The starling Applied to a brunette's vulva.
The crack It is like a crack in a wall, and is devoid of flesh.
The crested one This is provided with a comb like a cock's which stands up at the moment of pleasure.
The snub-nosed This has thin lips and a tiny tongue.
The hedgehog This is where the skin is harsh and the hair coarse.
The taciturn This is the one which is sparing in words. Should a member penetrate a hundred times a day it would say nothing but would be content to look on.
The squeezer So called because of its squeezing action on the member. Immediately after penetration it starts to squeeze the member and draws it in with such gusto that were it possible, it would absorb the testicles too.
The importunate This is the vulva which will spare no member. If one spend a hundred

*'Know that there are eight things which favour coition: health, freedom
from worry, absence of preoccupation, a gay disposition, a generous diet, wealth
— and a variety in the features and complexion of the women.'*

nights with it and penetrated a hundred times a night, it would neither be tired nor satisfied, but would rather ask for more. With it, the roles are inverted: the member is the defender, and it the petitioner. However, it is very rare, being only found in those women who are all flame and fire.

The sprinkler During urination this makes a loud rustling noise.

The desirer This is only met with in a few women; in some it is a natural gift, in others it is the result of prolonged abstinence. Its distinguishing feature is that it seeks out the member, and when it has found it, it refuses to release it until its fire is quenched.

The beauty This name is given to the white plump vulva which is rounded like a dome. The eye cannot quit it, and no member can withstand it.

The sweller So called because, when a member arrives at the entrance, it is caused to swell and stand up at once. It procures enormous satisfaction for its owner, and, at the moment of enjoyment, it winks.

The high-brow This is surmounted by a pubis which resembles a stately forehead.

The spreader So called because, at the approach of the member, it appears to be closed and impenetrable to such an extent that it would seem impossible to insert the little finger; but, when a member rubs it with its head, it widens considerably.

The giant This is as long as it is wide, that is, it is developed in both directions, from side to side and from the pubis to the perineum. It is the most beautiful that the eye may ever behold. May God in His goodness never deprive us of such a sight!

The glutton This is the one with a wide throat. If it has been deprived of coition for a certain time and a member should then approach it, it will swallow it whole, as a hungry man will throw himself on to food and try to swallow it without chewing.

The bottomless pit Applied to the vagina which is prolonged indefinitely. It necessitates the use of a very long member, no other being able to satisfy its desires.

The two-lipped one This is applied to the vulva of an exceedingly stout woman.

The camel's hump This is crowned by a mons veneris which stands out like a camel's hump and which stretches between the thighs like a calf's head. God grant that we may enjoy such a vulva! Amen!

The sieve When this vulva receives a member it starts to move up and down, right and left, backwards and forwards, until complete satisfaction.

The mover When this has received the member it moves violently and without interruption until the penis reaches the womb. It takes no rest until the operation is completely terminated.

The annexer That vagina is so called, which when it has received a member, clings round it as closely as possible, so that, if it could, it would draw in the testicles.

The accommodator This name is applied to the vagina of the woman who has felt for some time an ardent desire for coition. In its satisfaction at seeing a member, it aids it in its reciprocating movement; it eagerly offers the womb, and it could offer nothing more welcome. When the member wishes to visit any particular part it lends itself graciously to the task, so that no nook is left unvisited.

When enjoyment arrives and the member wishes to ejaculate, it clasps its head and presents the womb. It then vigorously sucks the member, using all its powers to extract the sperm destined to flow into the expectant womb. And, certainly, pleasure is incomplete for the woman possessing such a vagina if the flood of semen is not poured into the womb.

The helper This vulva is so called because it helps the member to enter and withdraw or to move up and down. By this help the ejaculation is easy and enjoyment complete. Even he who is ordinarily slow to ejaculate is vanquished by this vulva.

The arch This is a large-sized vulva.

The extender This name suits only a few vulvas. The one in question extends from the pubis to the anus. It lengthens when the woman is lying or standing, and shortens when she sits, differing thereby from the round form. It resembles a magnificent cucumber stretched between the thighs. It can sometimes be seen through light clothing when the woman leans backwards.

The duellist The vulva which, once the member is in, moves with it for fear it should be withdrawn before enjoyment is complete. It feels no pleasure unless the sucker is roused so that the member can be closely clasped. Certain vulvas, animated with a violent desire for coition, either natural or as the result of prolonged continence, move forward with open mouth to meet the member like a hungry child towards its mother's breast. It is thus that this vulva moves at the approach of a member, and they then resemble two skilful duellists: as the one precipitates itself on its adversary, this latter feints to frustrate the attack. The member may be likened to a sword and the vulva to a shield. The one which ejaculates first is the vanquished, and truly it is a final combat! So would I fight until my death!

The wet one This speaks for itself. Excessive secretion militates against enjoyment.

The barricaded one This is rarely met with. The fault which characterizes it is sometimes the result of circumcision badly performed.[12]

The abyss The one which is always gaping and whose end is out of sight and reach.

12. Female circumcision, clitorodectomy, is a mutilation still practised today by some peoples. It does not seem to have a ritual significance analogous to male circumcision, being explained by some practitioners as preventing masturbation and adultery.

Standing postures require more precise physical correspondence between partners than other love-making positions and were not favoured by Sheikh Nefzawi who recommends the position he calls 'pounding on the spot'. 'Prepare her for the enjoyment, and let nothing be neglected to attain this end.'

The biter The one which, when the member has penetrated, burns with such passion that it opens and shuts on the member. Especially at the moment of ejaculation the man feels his member seized by the sucker which draws like a magnet and exhausts it of its sperm. If God in his power has decreed that the woman shall conceive, the sperm is concentrated in the woman, but, if not, it is expelled.

The sucker This is the vagina which, dominated by amorous ardour resulting from continence or frequent and voluptuous caresses, grasps the member and sucks it with a strength capable of draining its sperm, acting thus as a child who sucks its mother.

The wasp This vulva is known by the strength and hardness of the pubic hair. When the member approaches it gets stung as by a wasp.

The ever-ready This name is given to the vagina of a woman passionately fond of the virile member. It is the one which, far from being intimidated by a hard and stiff penis, treats it with contempt and demands one harder.

It is also the one which is neither frightened nor ashamed when someone raises the clothes which cover it; on the contrary, it gives the member the warmest welcome, lets it rest on the dome and, not content with giving it a seat on the pubis, puts it inside and buries it so completely that the testicles cry: 'Oh, what a misfortune! Our brother had disappeared. He has plunged boldly into this gulf and we fear greatly for him. He must be the bravest of the brave to dash like that into a cavern!' The vagina, hearing their cries and wishing to allay their fears as to the disappearance of their brother, exclaims: 'Have no fear for him, he is still alive and hears your cries.' Then they reply: 'If what you say is true, let him come out that we may see him.' 'I shall not let him come out alive,' says the vulva. The testicles then ask what crime he has committed that he must be put to death – would not prison or the bastinado suffice? The vulva replies: 'By the existence of Him Who created Heaven, he shall only come out dead!' . . . then, addressing the member, it says: 'Do you hear your brothers' words? Make haste and show yourself to them for your absence afflicts them.' As soon as it has ejaculated, the member, reduced to nothing, appears to them, but they refuse to recognize it, saying: 'Who are you, oh flabby phantom?' 'I am your brother, and I was ill,' it replies; 'did you not see what state I was in before I entered? I called on all the doctors to consult them, but what a doctor I found there! He has treated my complaint and cured me without the need of examining me.' The testicles reply: 'Oh brother, we suffer the same as you, for we are one with you. Why did not God wish us to follow a treatment? With that, the semen flows into them and augments their volume. Wishing to be treated for their illness, they say: 'Oh dear friend, make haste and take us to the doctor that he may treat us. He will know what to do, for he understands all diseases.'

The fleer It is the organ of most virgins who, not yet acquainted with the member and seeing it approach, do all they can to keep it away when it insinuates itself between their thighs to force a way in.

The resigned The one which, having received the member, patiently endures any movement it may like to make. It is also the one which can resignedly bear the longest and most violent copulations. The hundredth time finds it still resigned and, far from complaining, it gives thanks to God. It is equally resigned when visited by several different members in succession. It is generally found in women of ardent temperament; if they had their way the man would never withdraw.

The warmer This is one of the most praiseworthy of vulvas. The pleasure of coition is measured by the degree of heat set up.

The delicious one It is reputed to procure an unequalled pleasure, only comparable to that experienced by wild beasts and birds of prey, and for which they will fight to the death. And if it is so with animals, what must it be with man! Wars have no other cause but the search for the volupty which this vulva procures, and which is the

*Sheikh Nefzawi, in the Arab tradition, asserts that men's
desires 'are never so strong as women's'.*

supreme pleasure of life. It is a foretaste of the joys which await us in paradise, and only surpassed by the sight of God Himself.

It would to possible to find other names applicable to the female organs, but the number given strikes me as sufficient.

Concerning the Things which make the Generative Act Enjoyable

Know, oh Vizier (God grant you His mercy!), that the things which tend to develop a passion for coition are six in number: an ardent love, an abundance of sperm, the propinquity of the person loved, beauty of face, a suitable diet, and contact.

The extreme pleasure which has its source in an impetuous and abundant ejaculation depends on one circumstance; it is imperative that the vagina be capable of suction. It then clings to the member and sucks out the semen by an irresistible attraction which is only comparable to that of a magnet. Once the member is grasped by the sucker, the man can no longer prevent the emission of semen, and the member is tightly held until it is completely drained. However, if the man ejaculates before arousing the sucker, he derives but little pleasure from the act.

Know that there are eight things which favour coition: health, freedom from worry, absence of preoccupation, a gay disposition, a generous diet, wealth, and variety in the features and complexion of the women.

Wherein the Work is Terminated

Know, oh Vizier (may God grant you His mercy!), that this chapter contains all the most useful information a man of any age can need concerning the best ways of augmenting the sexual powers.

Hear what the wisest and most learned Sheikh has to say to the children of the Most High!

He who will eat every day, after fasting, the yolks of several eggs, will find in this aliment an energetic stimulant of the sexual powers. The same may be said of a diet of yolks and chopped onions continued for three days.

He who will boil some asparagus and then fry it in fat, adding some yolks and powdered condiments, and will eat of this dish every day, will find his desires and powers considerably strengthened.

He who will peel some onions and will put them in a stewpot with condiments and aromatics, then fry this mixture with oil and yolks, will acquire, if he eats some of it during several days, a vigour for coition which will surpass all idea and evaluation.

Camel's milk mixed with honey, if drunk habitually develops an astonishing vigour and keeps the member in erection all day and night.

He who will feed for several days on eggs cooked with myrrh, cinnamon and pepper, will find an increased vigour in his erections and in his capacity for coition. His member will be in such a turgid state that it will seem as if it could never return to a state of repose.

He who wishes to operate a whole night through and who, owing to the suddenness

'Any posture is unsatisfactory if kissing is impossible. . . .'

of the desire, has not been able to make the preparations I have already mentioned, will have recourse to the following: he will fry a good number of eggs in fresh fat and butter and, when they are well cooked, he will mix them with honey. If he will eat as much as possible of this with a piece of bread, he will be able to soothe and comfort all through the night.

There are also other drinks of excellent value of which the following is one: Mix a measure of the expressed juice of onions with two measures of clarified honey. Warm over a slow fire until the onion juice has disappeared and only the honey remains. Take off the fire and let cool, then put it by till needed. An ounce of this is mixed with three ounces of water and, in this, pigeon peas are soaked for twenty-four hours. This is drunk in winter and at night, just before going to bed—a single small dose only being taken. During that night there will be no repose for the member of the man who takes it. If a dose is taken for several consecutive days, the member will remain continuously rigid. A man of ardent temperament should not use the remedy as it may bring on an attack of fever. It is inadvisable to take this remedy for more than three days running, unless one is old or of a cold temperament—in no case should it be taken in summer.

In writing this book I have sinned indeed!
Your pardon, oh Lord, I surely shall need;
But, if on the last day you absolve me, why then,
All my readers will join me in a loud   AMEN!